How to
Teach Art
to Children

How to **Teach Art** to Children *is designed to increase children's awareness of the different kinds of art. It gives children a wide range of experiences and helps them to appreciate the art around them. Most importantly, it lets them know that there is no wrong way to do art.*

Art is… painting, drawing, pasting, sculpting. It's sewing and building, coloring and folding. It is expressing and observing. Art is getting something that is inside you outside you.

Contents

Materials Lists

Variety of papers

colored construction paper— full-sized sheets, scraps

paper bags

tissue and toilet paper

wallpaper

wrapping paper

cardboard

newspaper

magazines

tagboard

Artists' tools

scissors

paste

glue

stapler

tape

hole punch

paintbrushes

rulers

Variety of craft supplies

straws

pipe cleaners

craft sticks

string

yarn

material scraps

buttons

dried beans

Painting supplies

tempera paint in assorted colors

watercolor trays

sponges for printing

gadgets for printing

trays or plates for mixing new colors

How to Teach Art to Children • EMC 1016 • © Evan-Moor Corp.

Words to Know

Complementary Colors: colors that are straight across from each other on the color wheel

Contrast: the use of light colors next to dark colors

Cool Colors: colors that have cool undertones: green, blue, and purple

Diagonal: a slanted line

Form: a three-dimensional object

Geometric Shape: a shape that fits into mathematics (circle, square, rectangle, triangle, etc.)

Horizon Line: a horizontal line used to represent the horizon in a one-point perspective drawing

Horizontal: a straight line that runs side to side

Hue: a color on the color wheel

Line: a basic element of art; the path made by a moving point

Monochromatic: an image with only one color

Organic Shape: a shape that comes from nature and does not fit into mathematics

Parallel Lines: two lines that run next to each other and never intersect

Primary Colors: colors that cannot be made by mixing other colors: red, yellow, and blue

Secondary Colors: colors that are made by mixing two primary colors: orange, green, and purple

Shade: a variety of a particular color with black added

Shape: a basic element of art; an area that is made by a line that touches at the beginning and end

Tertiary Colors: colors that are made by mixing one primary and one secondary color. These colors tend to be grayish. The primary color is always listed first: red-orange, yellow-orange, yellow-green, blue-green, blue-purple, red-purple.

Tint: a variety of a particular color with white added

Value: the use of lights and darks in artwork

Vanishing Point: the single point at which all images vanish in a one-point perspective drawing

Vertical: a straight up-and-down line

Warm Colors: colors that have warm undertones: red, orange, and yellow

Part One

Contents

Learning About the Elements of Art

The activities in Part One introduce the seven basic elements of art. Each section begins with a definition of the element. Each section also provides a series of art experiences that allow young artists to experiment with the element.

How to Use Part One

Preview the Element Before you teach children about an art element, read the definition on the introductory page at the beginning of each section. Think about the element in terms of the following questions:

- Is the element part of your everyday perception?
- How would your world be different without the element?
- Have you ever used the element to express yourself?

Share the Definition

Share the definition with children. After reading the definition, you may wish to have children look at literature illustrations and art examples to find uses of the element.

Share Fine Art Examples

Share fine art examples with children. Ask students to look thoughtfully at the art and name the things they think contribute to its overall impression. You may ask questions such as:

- What is this art showing?
- Is it a happy picture or an unhappy picture?
- What story do you think the artist is trying to tell?
- Does something in the picture make it seem real?

Describe the Art Experiences

Describe the experiences to children. Tell them the step-by-step directions for completing an activity, but do not make a sample and expect children's work to look like it. This is a time to encourage creativity.

The Art Experiences

The art experiences are designed to encourage children to explore materials and techniques rather than to simply complete projects.

Display Children's Art

Display children's art to validate their efforts and creativity. As children view their artwork, discuss the art element and the evidence of its use in the completed projects.

Line

Learning About

Line

Lines have names that describe their place in space. They may be diagonal, vertical, or horizontal. Lines may be thick or thin, solid or broken. When two lines sit next to each other, they become parallel lines. Lines can be bent into curves and broken into angles.

Line

Lines of All Kinds

Lines have names that describe their place in space. They may be diagonal, vertical, or horizontal. Lines may be thick or thin, solid or broken. When two lines are the same distance apart for their entire length, they are parallel.

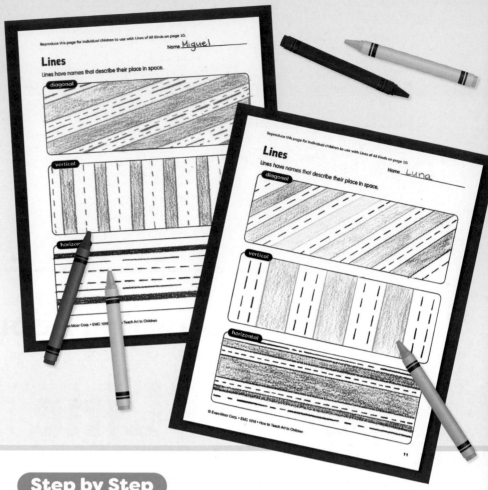

Materials

- crayons or pencils
- page 11, reproduced for each child

Step by Step

1. Have children look around and name examples of lines that they observe.

2. Introduce the words **diagonal**, **vertical**, and **horizontal** as ways of describing lines in space.

3. Next, give children page 11 and have them draw one line of each type in the boxes.

4. Then have them draw another line parallel to each of the original lines.

5. Ask the children to shade in the area between the two parallel lines. They will have created a thick line out of two thin lines.

6. Then have the children add broken lines in each area.

7. Finally, have them complete their designs by adding more lines and color.

Reproduce this page for individual children to use with Lines of All Kinds on page 10.

Name ____________________

Lines

Lines have names that describe their place in space.

diagonal

vertical

horizontal

Line

Line Designs

Children plan a design to reinforce their understanding of diagonal, vertical, and horizontal lines.

Materials

- white shelf paper—
  1 yard (.9 m)
- assorted colored
  construction paper
  strips—1/2" x 12"
  (1.3 x 30.5 cm)
- felt-tip pens
- glue
- scissors

Step by Step

1. Give children the paper supplies and pens.

2. Have them use a black pen to divide their white paper into three areas. They may divide the paper into squares, overlapping shapes, or equal parts.

3. Then have children glue cut-paper lines to each area. The lines may be thick, thin, solid, or broken.

   - One area should contain only diagonal lines.

   - One area should contain only vertical lines.

   - One area should contain only horizontal lines.

4. Children may want to draw lines with a felt-tip pen to enrich their designs.

Line

Curves and Angles

Lines can be bent into curves and broken into angles. In this way, lines can create an infinite number of configurations.

Step by Step

1. Discuss the different types of lines that can be created by changing a straight line into one that bends or curves.

   - zigzag
   - wavy
   - looped
   - curly
   - scalloped

2. Then give children the construction paper and have them fold their papers into eight equal rectangles.

3. Invite them to create a different type of line in each box.

Materials

- white construction paper—9" x 12" (23 x 30.5 cm)
- crayons

Line

Curved or Bent?

Children combine curved lines and straight lines to create interesting designs.

Materials

- white construction paper—6" (15 cm) squares
- large piece of black poster paper
- crayons or felt-tip pens
- glue

Step by Step

1. Give children the white squares.
2. On three of the squares, have children draw only straight, bent, and angular lines to create a design.
3. On the other squares, have children draw only curved lines to create a design.
4. After they finish drawing their designs, glue the squares to the black paper.

Line

Line Delight
Children use lines to form the basis for a design.

Step by Step

1. Give children the white paper and pens or markers.

2. Then challenge them to create a design that begins with two black lines.

   - The lines may be horizontal, vertical, or diagonal.

   - Both lines must travel in the same direction.

   - The lines do not need to be parallel. One line may be curved and the other bent.

3. Children should create three or more different designs to complete the challenge.

4. They can add color to their designs.

5. After they finish drawing their designs, have children glue them to the black construction paper.

Materials

- white construction paper—4" x 5" (10 x 13 cm)

- black construction paper—9" x 12" (23 x 30.5 cm)

- permanent black felt-tip pens or colored markers

- glue

Line

Create a Maze

Children tear three blobs from a rectangle and outline the blobs with a continuous line to fill the rectangle.

Materials

- white paper—8 1/2" x 11" (21.5 x 28 cm)
- bright-colored paper— 9" x 12" (23 x 30.5 cm)
- fine-tip marking pens
- glue

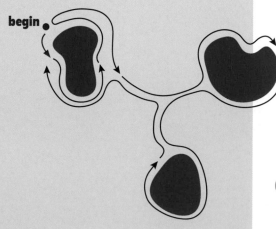

Step by Step

1. Give children the white paper and pens.

2. Have them fold small sections of the white paper and tear out three interesting shapes. (Younger children may choose to glue irregular shapes to the white paper instead of tearing out pieces.)

3. Then have them use a fine-tip marking pen to draw a circular line around one of the torn shapes (holes).

   - Before that line comes to completion, have children draw toward the next shape.

   - Circle around the second shape, then draw toward the third shape. Continue the line until you have filled the paper.

   - **The objective is to draw one continuous line.** Children cannot cross over a line, but they may make a U-turn and go backwards.

4. After children finish, mount their mazes on bright-colored paper.

Curved-Line Bookmark

Children cut narrow strips of construction paper in a curve and layer the strips to create a bookmark.

Step by Step

1. Have children choose three different colored strips.

2. Then have them cut each strip into two pieces with a curved cut.

3. Next, guide children to layer the pieces to create a bookmark. The straight end should always be placed toward the bottom of the bookmark.

4. Have children glue the pieces together.

5. You may wish to laminate the bookmarks.

Materials

- 3" x 6" (7.5 x 15 cm) colored construction paper strips

- scissors

- glue

a

b

c

d

e

f

Shape

How to Teach Art to Children • EMC 1016 • © Evan-Moor Corp.

Learning About

Shape

Lines create the outline of shapes. Each time a line outlines a shape, it is really creating two images: a positive one and a negative one.

Shape

Lines Outline Shapes

Children create the outline of shapes using lines.

Materials

- newsprint or other drawing paper
- pencils

Step by Step

1. Give children the paper and pencils and invite them to sketch along with you.

2. Draw a circle, a square, and a triangle. Point out that these shapes are made up of curved or bent lines. Each is a familiar basic shape that is created by connecting lines.

3. Look at simple objects such as an apple, a bottle, or a vase. Draw an outline of the shapes. (This form of drawing is called contour or outline drawing.)

   - Only the outline of the object is drawn.

   - No inside details are added.

> **Note:** *Keep the pencil on the paper while drawing. The resulting drawing may be distorted and exaggerated, but it emphasizes that form is an outline in space that can be manipulated as it is drawn.*

A Shape Design

Children create a design using felt shapes and then copy the design onto paper.

Step by Step

1. Give children the flannel board and felt shapes.

2. Then have them manipulate the felt shapes to create abstract designs on the flannel board. They should experiment with many different designs to see which ones they like the best.

3. Next, give children the drawing paper and crayons and have them draw the designs they made with the felt shapes.

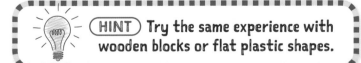

HINT Try the same experience with wooden blocks or flat plastic shapes.

Materials

- a flannel board
- felt shapes, 3 colors each:
  circles—red, blue, and yellow
  squares—red, blue, and yellow
  triangles—red, blue, and yellow
  rectangles—red, blue, and yellow
- drawing paper
- red, blue, and yellow crayons

Shape

Positive and Negative Shapes

Every time a line outlines a shape, it is really creating two images: the positive one that is outlined and the negative one that is the background.

Materials

- construction paper in strong, contrasting colors—6" (15 cm) squares
- glue
- scissors

Step by Step

1. Give each child a square of paper.

2. Have children fold the squares in half once and cut a shape out of the center. They now have a positive and a negative representation of a shape.

3. Next, have children choose a paper square of a contrasting color. Have them glue the positive shape they cut out to the paper square.

4. Post the squares around the edge of a bulletin board, window, or chalkboard. Enjoy the shapes!

Shape Designs

Children draw patterns inside a positive shape to create a large, bold design.

Step by Step

1. Give children the white construction paper. Have them draw a large circle, square, triangle, or more complicated contour drawing on the white construction paper.

2. Then have them fold the paper in half and cut out the symmetrical shape.

3. Tell children to draw a pattern inside the shape. They can:

   • divide the shape into several parts.

   • fill each part with a different design or pattern.

4. After children finish drawing their designs, mount the shapes on colored pieces of construction paper.

Materials

- white construction paper—12" x 18" (30.5 x 46 cm)

- assorted colors of construction paper—12" x 18" (30.5 x 46 cm)

- glue

- scissors

- crayons or felt-tip pens

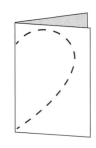

Shape

Shape Search

Some shapes, particularly those used in mathematics, fit definitions and can be given a name. Some shapes are irregular and don't fit a definition. Circles, ovals, crescents, squares, rectangles, triangles, and trapezoids are named shapes. A paint spill might be an irregular shape that doesn't fit a definition.

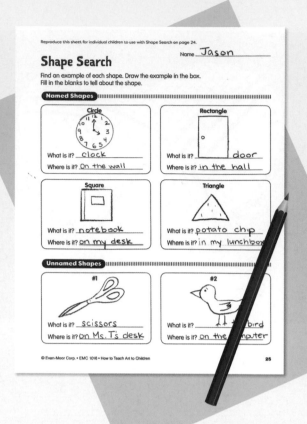

Materials

- page 25, reproduced for each child
- crayons or pencils

Step by Step

1. Give children a copy of the Shape Search on page 25.

2. Have them find and name shapes in their environment.

3. Then have them draw examples or take photos of the shapes.

4. Lastly, have them tell someone about the shapes they found.

Shape Search

Name _____

Find an example of each shape. Draw the example in the box.
Fill in the blanks to tell about the shape.

Named Shapes |||||||||||||||||||||||||||||||||||||||||||||||||||||||||||||||||||||||||||||||||||

Circle

What is it? _____

Where is it? _____

Rectangle

What is it? _____

Where is it? _____

Square

What is it? _____

Where is it? _____

Triangle

What is it? _____

Where is it? _____

Unnamed Shapes ||||||||||||||||||||||||||||||||||||||||||||||||||||||||||||||||||||||||||||||||

#1

What is it? _____

Where is it? _____

#2

What is it? _____

Where is it? _____

Shape

What Is It?

Each child uses the same shape and creates a picture incorporating the shape. Pictures are compared to document the variety of results.

Materials

- construction paper—
  blue 2" (5 cm) circles
  white 6" (15 cm) squares

- glue

- crayons

Step by Step

1. Give children the blue paper circles and the white paper squares.

2. Then have children glue one blue circle on one white square.

3. Next, have children draw lines to complete a picture. The blue circle must be a part of the picture.

4. Lastly, have children share their thoughts about the completed pictures and talk about the different things the blue circles represent.

 HINT Extend this project by using different shapes and colors in the project. Older children may enjoy the challenge of using several shapes at the same time.

Shape

A Shape Collage

Children cut two identical shapes into pieces. Then they put the pieces back together and create a collage.

Step by Step

1. Have children choose two scraps of wrapping paper that are about the same size.

   a. Then have them hold the two pieces together as they cut out a square, triangle, or circle.

   b. and c. Next, have them hold the two identical shapes together, fold the shape in half, and cut out the center of the shape.

   d. Have children make additional cuts to the shape.

2. Lastly, children glue the pieces onto a construction paper square using parts of one colored shape to complete the other colored shape.

Materials

- 9" (23 cm) square of construction paper
- scraps of wrapping paper
- scissors
- glue

a.

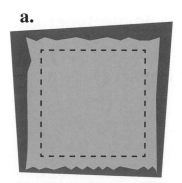

b.

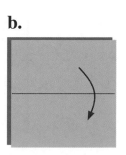

c.

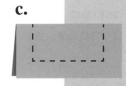

d.

Color

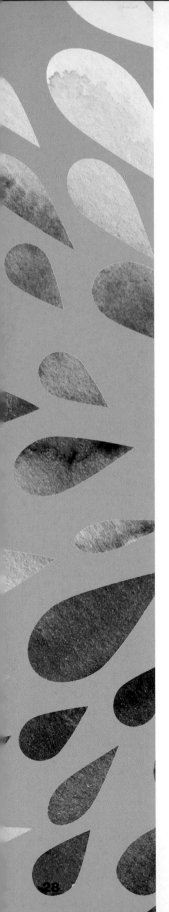

How to Teach Art to Children • EMC 1016 • © Evan-Moor Corp.

Learning About

Color

Color is a sensation produced by various rays of light of different wavelengths.

Color

Primary Colors

There are three primary colors: red, yellow, and blue. These colors are called primary colors because you can mix them to create all the colors of the rainbow. The colors create the foundation of the color wheel.

Materials

- miscellaneous objects in the three primary colors
- a colorful environment

Step by Step

1. Show children objects that have the three primary colors. Then have them brainstorm things associated with each color.

   yellow—sun, lemons, flowers, school buses
   blue—sky, water, jeans
   red—apples, fire, roses, sunsets, hearts

2. Discuss how each color has certain feelings associated with it.

   yellow—cheerful
   blue—cool or sad
   red—angry or hot

3. Invite children to look around the room and identify red objects. Ask, "Does red look the same each time?"

4. Take a red sweater and compare how light or dark the red seems to be depending on whether it is located in a dark closet or out in the sunlight. Help children conclude that any color may be altered by the amount of light that surrounds it.

A Primary Color Quilt Design

Children create paper quilts using primary-colored squares.

Step by Step

1. Give children the paper supplies.

2. Have them place the larger primary-colored paper squares on the butcher paper.

> **Note:** *Encourage children to experiment with different color arrangements. There is no "correct" way to arrange the colors.*

3. Next, have the children place the smaller paper squares on top of the large squares. They may want to try many combinations before they decide on the final arrangement.

4. Lastly, have children glue all the squares in place.

Materials

(for each child)

- construction paper—
  - 9" (23 cm) squares:
    three blue
    three red
    three yellow
  - 3" (7.5 cm) squares:
    three blue
    three red
    three yellow
- butcher paper—
  27" (69 cm) square folded
  into 9" (23 cm) squares
- glue

Color

One-Color Art

Children create simple drawings with one primary color.

Materials

(for each child)

- construction paper— three white 12" (30.5 cm) squares
- red, yellow, and blue crayons
- black crayon or felt-tip pen (optional)

Step by Step

1. Give each child three white squares of paper and the drawing tools.

2. Then challenge children to draw three objects or pictures. They should use only one primary color for each picture. (Black may be used to outline or add details to each of the pictures.)

3. After children finish their drawings, display pictures of the same color together. For example, hang all of the red drawings together.

4. Then ask children about the drawings:

   - What do the red drawings have in common? What is different about them?

   - How do you feel when you look at the blue pictures? How do you feel when you look at the yellow pictures?

Three-Color Paint Job

Children paint pictures using the three primary colors.

Step by Step

1. Write each painting challenge on a notecard. Put the paper, paints, and paintbrushes on a table for children.

2. Have children choose a challenge and use the three primary colors to paint a picture.

3. After children finish painting, have them talk about what they noticed when they used the primary colors together.

Materials

- large white painting paper
- red, yellow, and blue tempera paints
- paintbrushes in a variety of sizes
- painting challenges written on notecards

Painting Challenges

- *Paint a beach ball rolling into the sea.*
- *Paint a rowboat on the lake on a sunny day.*
- *Paint red, blue, and yellow fruit.*
- *Paint an airplane zooming over a circus tent.*
- *Paint a watering can in a flower garden.*
- *Paint a child with an umbrella walking in the rain.*
- *Paint a wind vane on the top of a barn.*
- *Paint a child with a wagon.*

Color

Design a Flag

Children create flags using the three primary colors.

Materials

(for each child)

- construction paper—
  white 9" x 12" (23 x 30.5 cm)
  red 6" (15 cm) square
  blue 6" (15 cm) square
  yellow 6" (15 cm) square

- glue

- scissors

- black crayon (optional)

Step by Step

1. Give children the paper, the glue, and the scissors.

2. Then have them plan and design flags using the three primary colors. They may cut the three primary-colored squares into any shape.

3. Encourage children to experiment and try several different designs before gluing the pieces in place.

4. After they finish gluing, they may wish to use a black crayon to add details to their flag.

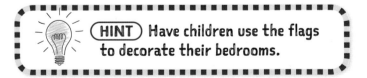

HINT Have children use the flags to decorate their bedrooms.

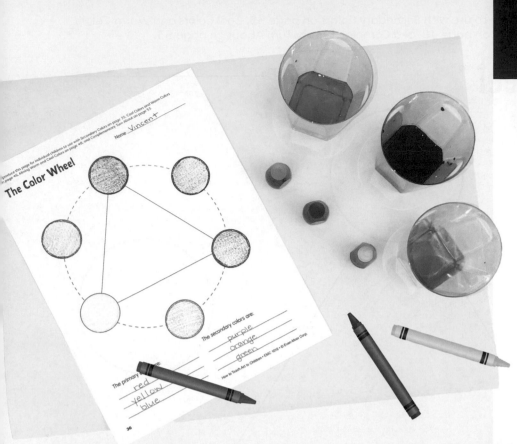

Secondary Colors

Primary colors can be mixed to create the secondary colors of orange, green, and purple.

Step by Step

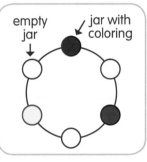

empty jar / jar with coloring

1 Place the three small jars of primary colors in the positions shown on the color wheel. Add three empty jars in the positions of the secondary colors.

2 Use eyedroppers to mix the primary colors to create secondary colors in the empty jars. Stir to mix. Begin with the lightest color and add the darker color one drop at a time.

3 When all the mixing is complete, you will have created the three secondary colors—purple, orange, and green.

4 Give children page 36 and colored pencils or crayons and have them complete the color wheel as shown above.

Note: *In this book the word* **purple** *is used instead of* **violet** *because* **purple** *is a color that is commonly found in crayons, construction paper, and paint.*

Materials

- food coloring and water premixed in glass jars for the three primary colors—red, blue, and yellow

- three glass jars for secondary colors

- three eyedroppers

- page 36, reproduced for each child

- colored pencils or crayons

Reproduce this page for individual children to use with Secondary Colors on page 35, Cool Colors and Warm Colors on page 46, Mixing Warm and Cool Colors on page 48, and Complementary Turn About on page 53.

The Color Wheel

Name _____

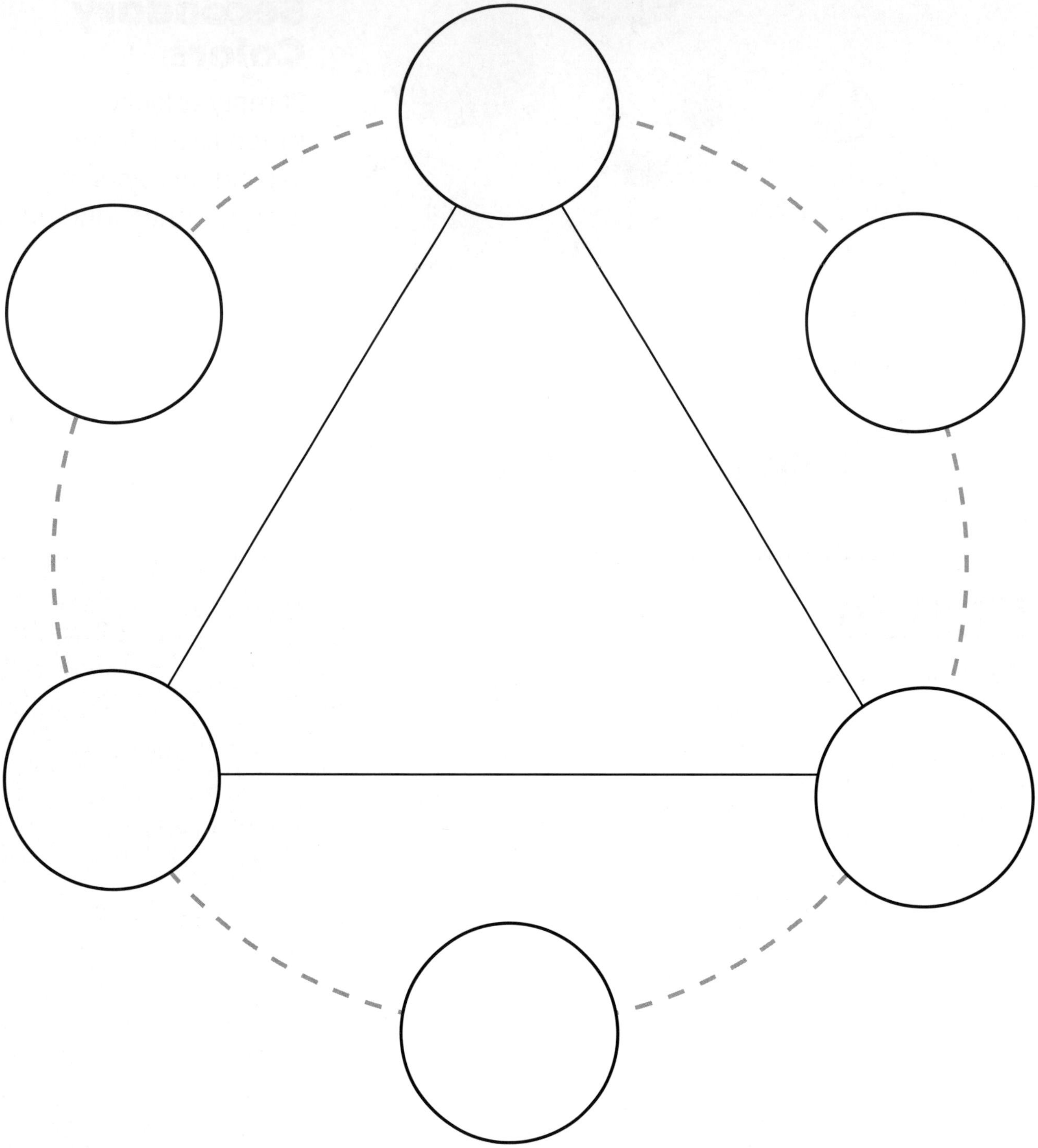

The primary colors are:

_____

_____

_____

The secondary colors are:

_____

_____

_____

Color Memory Game

This activity reinforces color memory and expands children's color awareness.

Step by Step

1 Cut the colored construction paper into strips and squares and write the same number on each matching color strip and square.

2 Put the strips in the container. Lay the squares, numbers facing down, in random order on a table.

3 Put a chair against the table with its seat facing away from the table. Have one child sit in the chair.

4 Hold the container of strips and have the child in the chair pick a colored strip from the container. He or she will read the number aloud and study the color before putting the strip back into the container.

5 The child then turns around and finds the matching color square on the table and reads the number to verify that it is the correct match.

Materials

- construction paper—several shades of every color
  - 2" x 6" (5 x 15 cm) strips
  - 4" (10 cm) squares to match the colored strips
- can or plastic container

HINT To make this game more challenging, use paint strips from the paint store in place of construction paper strips and squares.

Color

Color Mixing for All

Each child can experience the magic of color mixing in the art center.

Materials

- a pitcher of water
- six clear plastic cups
- a spoon
- small squeeze-type bottles of red, blue, and yellow food coloring
- page 39, reproduced for each child
- paper towels
- a plastic tub or sink for cleanup
- markers

Step by Step

1. Set up the color mixing center.

2. Have children visit the center and experiment with mixing the primary colors. Remind them to always begin with the lightest color and add the darker color one drop at a time.

3. Have children use markers to record the colors mixed on the sheet.

4. Challenge children to mix three colors and discover new shades.

 HINT For a sensory experience, blend small balls of brightly colored playdough.

Name _____

Color Experiments

Begin with the three primary colors.

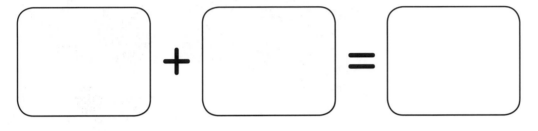

Color in the boxes to show what you have mixed.

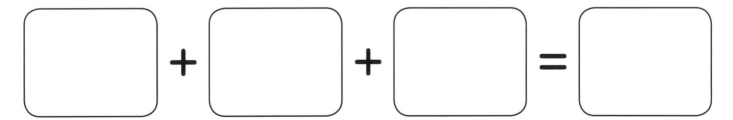

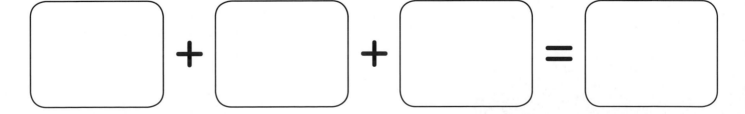

Color

Mixing Gradations of Color

Children discover that mixing different amounts of a color changes the color's hue.

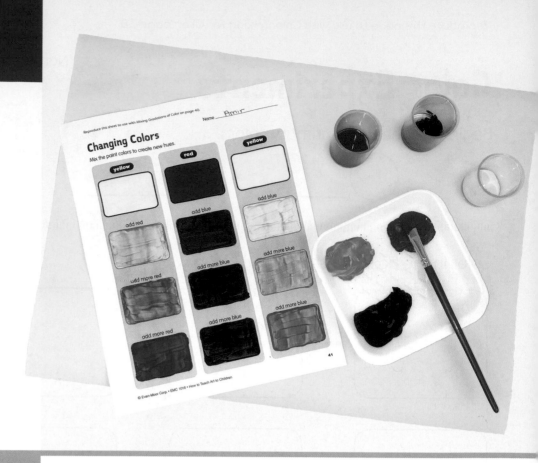

Materials

- tempera or watercolor paints
- paintbrushes
- plate or foam tray for mixing colors
- water and paper towels
- page 41, reproduced for each child

Step by Step

1. Give each child page 41, paints, a paintbrush, and a tray.

2. The children paint the first square on their paper and make a dab of the same color on the plate.

3. Then they follow the directions on page 41 to add more color. After mixing a new color on the tray, the child paints the square below the direction.

4. Children continue to mix and paint to fill in each square on their sheet.

5. Allow the sheets to dry completely.

 HINT Children may enjoy creating a picture using the colored squares from the sheet. The squares may be cut out and arranged in interesting designs on another sheet of paper.

Name _____

Changing Colors

Mix the paint colors to create new hues.

yellow	**red**	**yellow**
add red	add blue	add blue
add more red	add more blue	add more blue
add more red	add more blue	add more blue

Color

The Background Makes a Difference

Contrast is the degree of difference between colors or tones in a piece of artwork.

Materials

- a basket of small colorful objects
- colored construction paper—12" x 18" (30.5 x 46 cm)

Step by Step

1. Place the basket full of items and the construction paper on a table.

2. Have children choose an item and lay it on a colored background.

3. Then have children change the background to see if the item looks better with a different color. Ask: *Which combinations of color have the best contrast?*

4. Then give children an opportunity to share which color combinations are their favorites and why.

 HINT Create an interesting bulletin board. Use squares of different-colored construction paper as the background. Mount the same object on all the squares.

Color

Pick Contrasting Colors

Children manipulate colors to discover which colors make good contrasts.

Step by Step

1. Give each child the large and small construction paper squares and the crayons.

2. Have children lay out all six of the larger squares. Then have them place one of the smaller squares in the center of each larger one.

3. Children rearrange the smaller squares until they find the three best contrasting combinations. Then they use crayons to show those color combinations on page 44.

4. Next, children decide which three combinations of colors have the least contrast and show those choices on page 44.

5. Lastly, children record their favorite color combinations.

6. Invite children to discuss their choices.

Materials

(for each child)

- construction paper—

  six 5" (13 cm) squares of red, orange, yellow, green, blue, and purple

  six 2" (5 cm) squares of the same colors

- page 44, reproduced for each child

- crayons

Contrasting Colors

Name _____

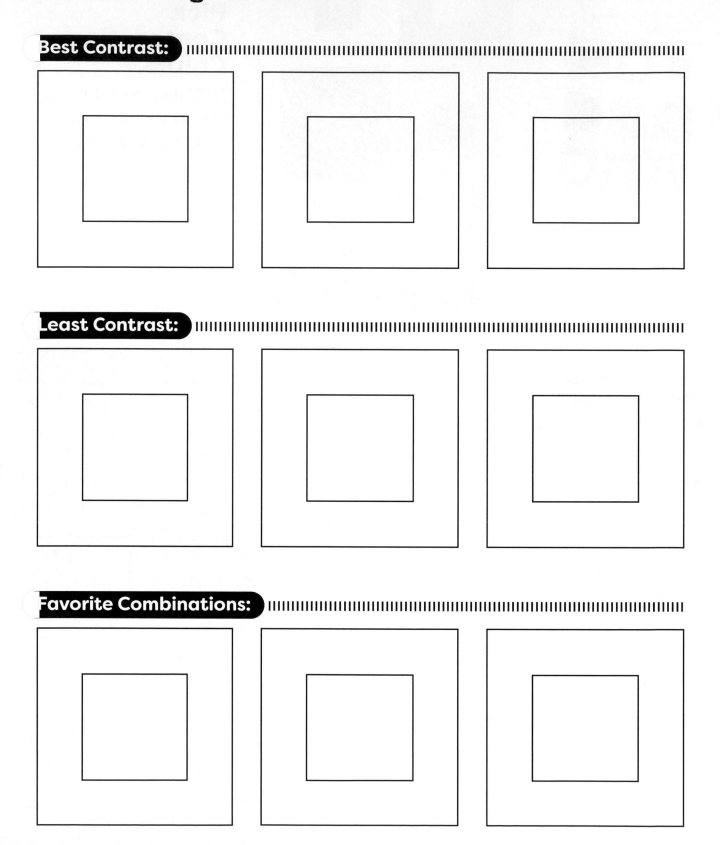

Best Contrast:

Least Contrast:

Favorite Combinations:

Contrasting Backgrounds

Children experience how contrasting colors affect their artwork. They will choose a background that creates the effect they desire.

Step by Step

1. Give each child the construction paper squares, a pencil, scissors, and glue.

2. Have children draw a shape on each of their smaller squares. Then have them cut out the shapes.

3. Guide children to experiment with background color by having them lay their cut-out shapes on several different colors of background paper.

4. Lastly, have children choose the colors they like best and glue the shapes to the background colors.

> **Notes:**
> *yellow on yellow = poor contrast*
> *yellow on purple = strong contrast*
> *yellow on red = good contrast, warm colors*

Materials

(for each student)

- colored construction paper—assortment of 6" (15 cm) and 3" (7.5 cm) squares

- a pencil

- scissors

- glue

Color

Cool Colors and Warm Colors

Blue, green, and purple are often labeled as cool colors. Yellow, orange, and red are called warm colors. Children categorize colors as cool and warm.

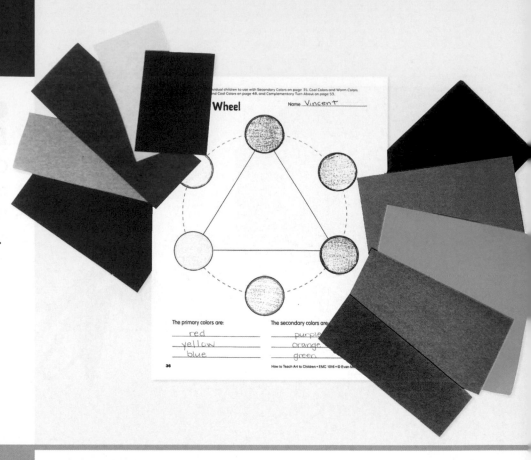

Materials

- *Owl Moon* by Jane Yolen
- *Arrow to the Sun* by Gerald McDermott
- colored paper scraps
- children's completed color wheels from page 36

Step by Step

1. Read the book *Owl Moon*. Discuss the illustrator's choice of colors to depict the moonlit winter night.

2. Read *Arrow to the Sun*. Discuss the illustrator's choice of colors.

3. Compare the colors used in the two books and the two different settings.

4. Give children the colored paper scraps and have them sort them into two piles:
   - colors that fit the cool winter setting of *Owl Moon*
   - colors that fit the warm desert setting of *Arrow to the Sun*

5. Then have them look at their color wheels and notice how they have been divided into cool colors and warm colors.

How to Teach Art to Children • EMC 1016 • © Evan-Moor Corp.

all warm

mostly cool

mostly warm

all cool

Colorful Collage

Children work with warm and cool colors to develop a collage.

Step by Step

1. Have children fold their butcher paper square into fourths. Label the sections of the paper: all warm, all cool, mostly warm (with a cool accent), mostly cool (with a warm accent).

2. Then have them search through magazines to find patches of color that fit one of the categories. Samples may be torn or cut from the magazines and glued in the correct section.

3. After children finish, have them compare their collages.

(HINT) Photographs with lots of white will not be as effective as solid-color photographs.

Materials

(for each child)

- magazines
- white butcher paper— 36" (91.5 cm) square
- scissors
- glue

Color

Mixing Warm and Cool Colors

Children experiment with color to create variations of the basic color wheel hues.

Materials

(for each child)

- tempera paints—red, yellow, blue, orange, green, and purple
- a paintbrush
- water
- plates or foam trays for mixing colors
- page 49, reproduced for each child

Step by Step

1. Give each child page 49, the paints, water, a paintbrush, and the trays.

2. Have children begin with the red row on page 49. They paint the first oval with red paint. Then they use a tray to mix a warm primary color with red to make a warmer red and paint the second oval with the warmer red.

3. Next, children add a cool primary color to red to make a cooler red and paint the second oval with the cooler red.

4. Children continue experimenting with each color on the color wheel.

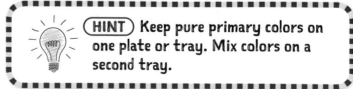

HINT Keep pure primary colors on one plate or tray. Mix colors on a second tray.

Name _____

Warm It Up—Cool It Down

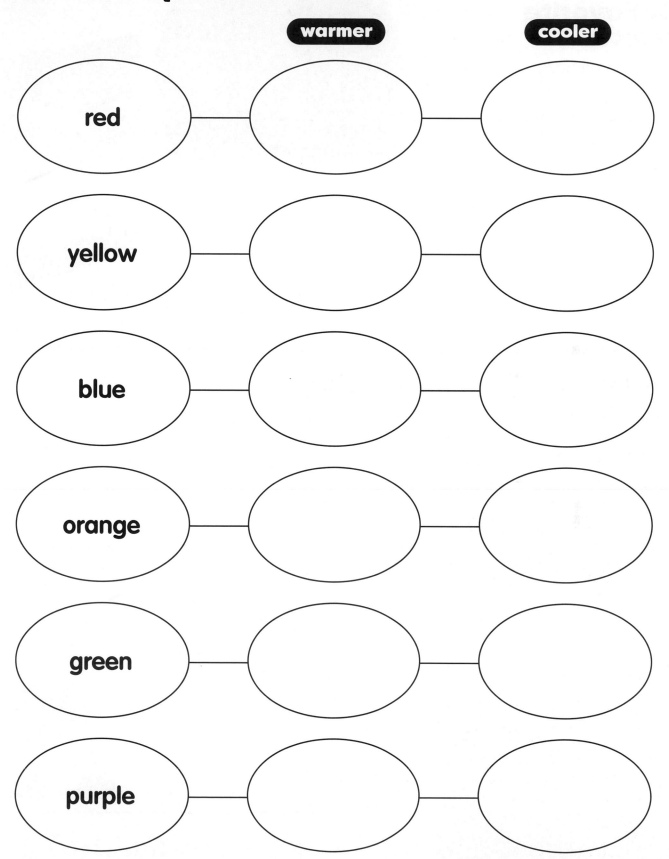

warmer   **cooler**

red

yellow

blue

orange

green

purple

Color

My Favorite Palette

After children have experimented with mixing variations of the primary and secondary colors, they choose a color combination that they especially like.

Materials

- paper for painting
- tempera paints
- paintbrushes
- water
- trays for mixing colors
- Pick a Palette painting task written on a notecard
- notecards

Step by Step

1. Set up the paper, paints, paintbrushes, water, and trays on a table. Place the painting task card on the table.

2. Have children choose their palettes and paint pictures using their chosen palettes.

3. Next, give children notecards and ask them to write about why they chose the palette they did.

4. Display the paintings and the notecards together.

> ### Pick a Palette:
> *Paint a picture with the palette you like the best.*
> - *Warm colors only*
> - *Cool colors only*
> - *Warm colors with a cool accent*
> - *Cool colors with a warm accent*

How to Teach Art to Children • EMC 1016 • © Evan-Moor Corp.

Complementary Colors

Complementary colors are pairs of colors that sit opposite one another on the color wheel.

Step by Step

1. Fold the butcher paper into 6" squares and then open it up and press it flat. Hang it on a wall.

2. Then give each child a 6" square and a 2" square of the colored construction paper in complementary colors.

3. Have children take turns pinning up the large colored squares onto the butcher paper. They may choose any available position for their squares.

4. Then have children take turns pinning their small squares within a large square of a complementary color. Small squares may be positioned anywhere within the larger squares: in the center, in a corner, etc.

Materials

- butcher paper— 36" (91.5 cm) square

- construction paper—
  - 6" (15 cm) squares: six each: red, orange, yellow, green, blue, and purple
  - 2" (5 cm) squares: six each: red, orange, yellow, green, blue, and purple

- straight pins

Complementary Rip and Paste

Children demonstrate that they can identify complementary colors as they create an abstract design.

Materials

(for each child)

- construction paper—

  white 9" x 12" (23 x 30.5 cm)

  4" (10 cm) squares— red, orange, yellow, green, blue, and purple

- glue

Step by Step

1. Explain to children that they will make a rip and paste design using colored construction paper. Tell them that the only rule they must follow is that only complementary colors may touch each other.

2. Then give children the white construction paper, the paper squares, and the glue.

3. Have children rip off a piece of each colored square. Then, remembering the rule, have children lay all the pieces on the white construction paper in a random design.

4. Children can add additional ripped pieces to create a pleasing design and then glue the pieces to the white construction paper.

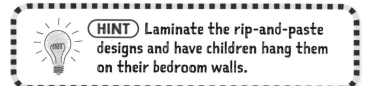

HINT Laminate the rip-and-paste designs and have children hang them on their bedroom walls.

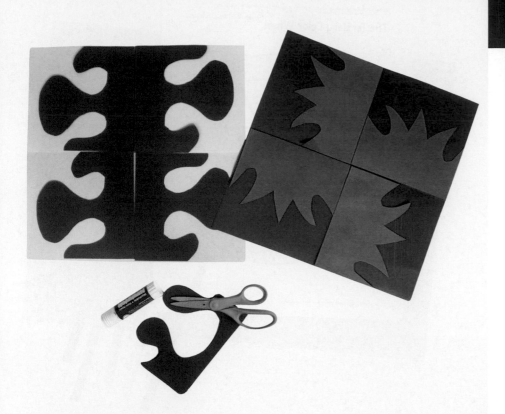

Complementary Turn About

This cut-and-paste project results in a striking design. Use it for the cover of a folder or portfolio.

Step by Step

1. Have children choose four 6" squares and a 12" square of complementary colors.

2. Then have them draw an interesting line across one of the 6" squares.

3. Next, holding the four small squares together, have children cut along the line.

4. Guide children to fold the 12" square into quarters and then open it up.

5. Lastly, children glue one of the cut pieces in each section of the larger square. The result is a design that is a striking use of complementary colors and a simple repetitive design.

Materials

(for each child)

- construction paper—

    four 6" (15 cm) squares— Provide a choice of all the colors on the color wheel.

    12" (30.5 cm) square— Provide a choice of all the colors on the color wheel.

- a pencil or marker
- glue
- scissors

Color

Tertiary Colors

Tertiary colors are colors created by the mixing of secondary colors. Mixing these hues tends to create colors with a grayish or muted effect.

Reproduce this color wheel to use with Tertiary Colors on page 54, Mixing to Match on page 56, and Colored Pencil Blending on page 57.

The Tertiary Color Wheel   Name _Ellie_

© Evan-Moor Corp. • EMC 1016 • How to Teach Art to Children   55

Materials

(for each child)

- page 55, reproduced for each child
- colored pencils or crayons in six colors on the color wheel
- a notebook
- a pencil

Step by Step

1. Give each child page 55 and the colored pencils.
2. Then have children color in the sections of the tertiary color wheel. They should blend the colors of the basic color wheel to make the tertiary colors.
3. Give children the notebooks and pencils and lead them on a walk around a neighborhood or other outdoor space. Help them identify tertiary colors in their environment.
4. Then have children use their notebooks to write and draw two examples by each color.

gray-green

yellow-green

blue-green

Reproduce this color wheel to use with Tertiary Colors on page 54, Mixing to Match on page 56, and Colored Pencil Blending on page 57.

The Tertiary Color Wheel

Name _____

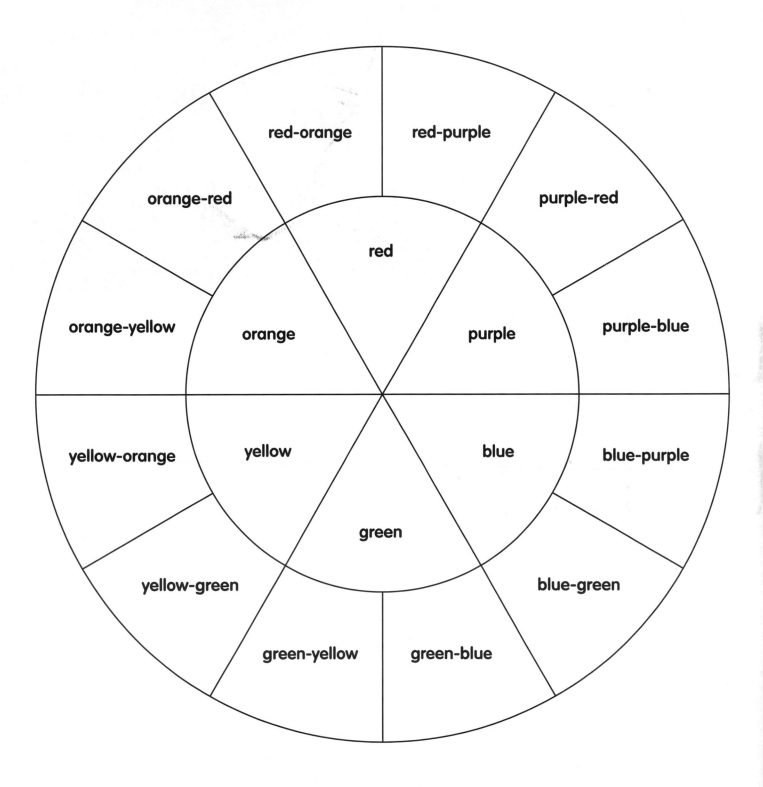

red-orange · red-purple · orange-red · purple-red · orange-yellow · purple-blue · red · purple · orange · yellow-orange · blue-purple · yellow · blue · green · yellow-green · blue-green · green-yellow · green-blue

Color

Mixing to Match

Children mix secondary colors to match the colors they see in nature.

Materials

- tempera paints—red, orange, yellow, green, blue, and purple
- white construction paper
- small items from home and nature that have muted colors—leaves, rocks, flowers, ribbons, figurines, etc.
- glue
- plates or trays
- paintbrushes
- water
- paper towels
- page 55, reproduced for each child (if it has not already been completed)
- colored pencils if needed

Step by Step

1. Have children take out their completed tertiary color wheel or use colored pencils to color the tertiary color wheel on page 55.

2. Then display the small items and have children choose four or five of them to use for color matching.

3. Next, have them lay each item beside the colors on the wheel to decide which colors are the best matches.

4. Then give children the white paper, water, paint, paintbrushes, and trays and have them mix the paint until they feel they have reached a good match for each small item.

5. Lastly, have children paint a sample splotch on the white paper and then glue the items next to the mixed colors.

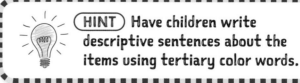

HINT Have children write descriptive sentences about the items using tertiary color words.

Colored Pencil Blending

Children find out how pencil layering of primary and secondary colors can achieve a muted, tertiary effect.

Step by Step

1. Give each child page 55 and the colored pencils.

2. Then have children use the colored pencils to complete the tertiary color wheel, layering one color over another. Guide them to apply light and consistent pressure on the pencil to achieve successful layering of color.

3. Display simple objects such as fruits, leaves, potted plants, or figurines as models for children.

4. Then have children create a picture of a simple object using the pencils and creating tertiary colors.

Materials

- colored pencils
- white drawing paper
- simple objects used as models
- page 55, reproduced for each child

Rainbow of Colors

Children build colorful mosaic pictures with paper scraps cut from magazines.

Materials

- white construction paper
- magazines
- scissors
- glue

Step by Step

1 Give children magazines and scissors and have them cut out small squares of colors from the pages.

2 Then have children divide the color squares into warm-color and cool-color piles. Next, have them separate those piles into more defined piles of secondary and tertiary colors.

3 After they have at least six piles (red, orange, yellow, green, blue, purple), give children white construction paper and have them glue the squares into place to form a design or a block letter that has been traced onto white paper.

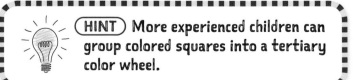

HINT More experienced children can group colored squares into a tertiary color wheel.

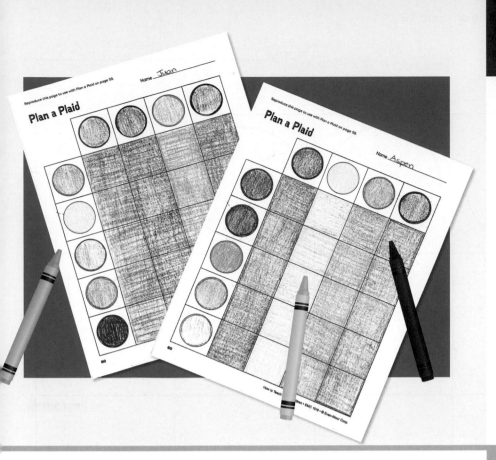

Plan a Plaid

Children create a plaid pattern by filling in a grid.

Step by Step

1. Give children page 60 and crayons.

2. Then have children choose a color for each of the four circles across the top of the page and color them in.

3. Next, have children color the five boxes below the first circle the same color as the first circle.

4. Then have children continue until all of the columns are colored to match each of the circles above.

5. Now have children choose a color for each of the five circles down the left side of the grid and color them.

6. Next, have children color the first horizontal row of boxes to match the first circle on the left. They have already colored those boxes once to match the top circles, so now they will be lightly placing another color over the top. It begins to lend an interesting plaid effect.

7. Lastly, have children color the next row and repeat the process until the whole page is finished.

Materials

- page 60, reproduced for each child

- crayons

Plan a Plaid

Name _____

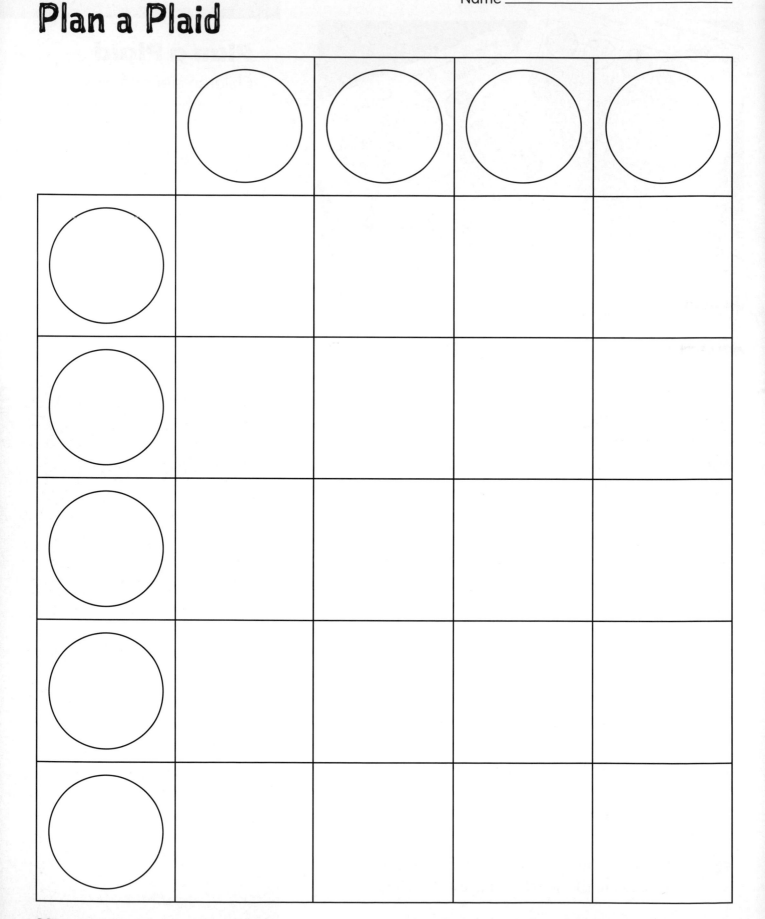

How to Teach Art to Children • EMC 1016 • © Evan-Moor Corp.

flashlight

box with slit

mirror

bowl of water

The Whole Spectrum

Children have first-hand experience creating their own rainbow of light using water and a mirror.

Step by Step

1. Have children assemble the materials as shown above.

2. Guide children to move the mirror to create a spectrum of light on the ceiling.

3. Have children discuss their results:

   • Were they able to create the spectrum in more than one way?

   • Was the intensity of colors different using different methods?

   • Why does the mirror work as a prism?

   • Are there other ways to create a spectrum of light?

4. Lastly, give each child page 62. Have children use the crayons to show the colors they observed.

Materials

• a tub or bowl of water

• a small mirror

• a flashlight

• cardboard box with a slit in the bottom

• page 62, reproduced for each child

• crayons or colored pencils

Notes: *Intermediate children need to know that light is made up of a band or a spectrum of color. These colors travel in waves, and each color has a different wavelength. You can prove this by letting light pass through a three-sided piece of glass called a prism. The light that appears clear is changed into seven colors as it passes through the prism: red, orange, yellow, green, blue, indigo, and violet.*

The Prism

Name _____

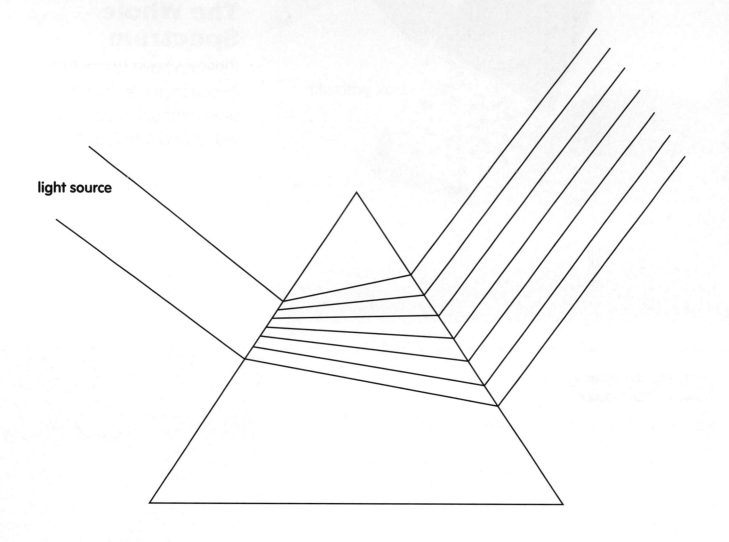

light source

What I observed

_____

_____

_____

_____

How to Teach Art to Children • EMC 1016 • © Evan-Moor Corp.

Prism Art

Children use what they have learned about the spectrum of colors to create a design.

Step by Step

1. Give children the construction paper, the crayons, and the pencils.

2. Have children draw a triangle in the center of the construction paper. This triangle represents a prism.

3. Then, beginning at the top, have children draw lines radiating from the triangle. Lines should be drawn in sets of seven similar lines, creating a section for each color in the spectrum.

4. Lastly, have children color in the design following the order in which the colors appear in the spectrum.

 HINT Cut out the designs and mount the cutouts on black paper. Discuss the way the eye is drawn to the center of the shape.

Materials

(for each child)

- white construction paper—12" x 18" (30.5 x 46 cm)
- crayons or felt-tip pens
- a pencil

Value

Learning About

Value

Any hue or color on the color wheel may have an infinite number of values or tones. When colors are used at full value, they appear strong and bright. When colors are mixed with white paint or water, they appear as muted, lighter tones.

Value

Black and White

Black and white offer a striking contrast when used together and create a strong visual image.

Materials

(for each child)

- construction paper—
  black 9" x 12"
  (23 x 30.5 cm)

  white 9" x 6"
  (23 x 15 cm)

- scissors
- glue
- a pencil

Step by Step

1. Give children the construction paper, pencils, scissors, and glue.

2. Have children draw several light pencil lines from the top to the bottom of the white paper.

3. Then have children cut the white paper on the pencil lines.

4. Next, guide children to spread out the white strips across the black paper. Encourage them to experiment with different designs.

5. Lastly, have children glue the white strips in place.

HINT Read <u>Black and White</u> by David Macaulay. Note the strong visual images that tell the story.

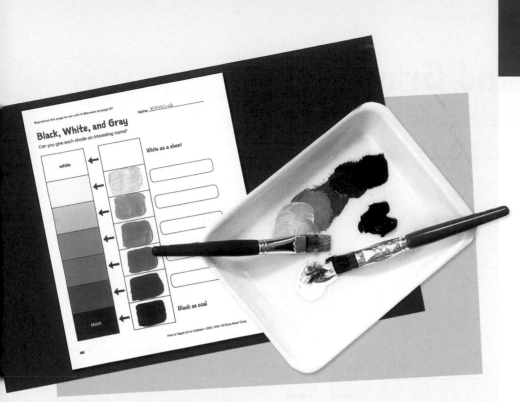

Value

In Between

Tones of gray exist between black and white. This activity involves the creation of a light-to-dark scale and requires careful mixing of colors.

Step by Step

1. Give each child page 68, the paints, water, paintbrush, and tray.

2. Have children begin by painting in the white box on page 68. Then have them paint the black box.

3. Next have children mix the middle tone. Tell them to put white on their plates and slowly add drops of black until they create the gray that they feel should be in the middle.

4. After painting the middle tone, children mix gradations of gray and fill in the other four boxes.

5. After children paint all of the boxes, challenge them to name each in-between color.

Materials

(for each child)

- tempera paints— white and black

- a paintbrush

- water for cleaning the paintbrush

- paper towels

- plate or foam tray

- page 68, reproduced for each child

Black, White, and Gray

Name _____

Can you give each shade an interesting name?

white		←		White as a sheet
gray		←		
gray		←		
gray		←		
gray		←		
gray		←		
black		←		Black as coal

Grays All Around

Children experiment with black, white, and gray paint.

Step by Step

1. Give children the paper, paints, paintbrushes, and trays.

2. Challenge children to think of an object or scene that could be gray. If they need some ideas, share the Painting Challenges listed below with them.

3. Then have children mix black and white paint to make various shades of gray.

4. Have children complete their pictures using only black, white, and gray.

> **Painting Challenges:**
> • *Snowman in a snowstorm*
> • *Cat on a foggy day*
> • *Cityscape at night*
> • *Train in a tunnel*
> • *Airplane in a cloud*

Materials

(for each child)

- tempera paints—black and white
- plate or foam tray
- a paintbrush
- white easel paper

Value

Colors Have Many Values

Children experiment with the values of colors.

Materials

(for each child)

- tray of watercolor paints
- large watercolor paintbrush
- butcher paper
- plate or dish
- cup of water

 HINT Have children compare the color to an emotion. A strong emotion like anger can be diluted to a muted emotion like irritation.

Step by Step

1. Give each child paper, a tray of watercolor paints, a plate, a cup of water, and a large watercolor paintbrush.

2. Have children create a colored puddle on their mixing plate using a full-strength primary color. Then have them paint a blotch of that same color on their paper.

3. Next, have children add a paintbrushful of water to the colored puddle on the plate—this will create a muted value of the first shade. Then have them paint a sample of that value on their paper.

4. Guide children to keep adding water and making blotches until the color ranges from a strong, pure value to a muted, pale value.

5. Have children repeat the steps, using a different color each time.

Value

Light and Dark

Children demonstrate that any color can have more than one value.

Step by Step

1. Give each child one piece of white paper and 8 different crayons.

2. Show children how to fold the construction paper into 16 squares.

3. Have children begin by picking a crayon and using it to color one of the boxes using a firm, solid stroke. Then have children use that same color to lightly shade in another box. The result should be a pale version of the original color.

4. Children continue coloring with all 8 crayons, one dark box and one pale box.

5. Give children the colored construction paper squares and the glue. Then show children how to create a frame for their design by gluing it to a colored construction paper square.

Materials

- construction paper—
  white 11" (28 cm) square
  colored 12" (30.5 cm) square
- box of crayons
- glue

Value

Mixing Colors with White

Colors mixed with white are called tints. This project encourages children to create tints of the color wheel colors.

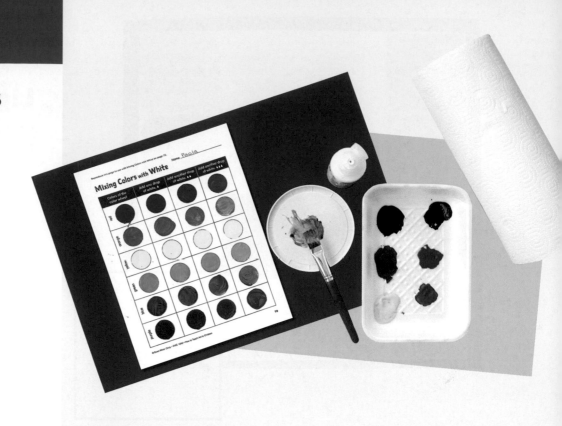

Materials

- tempera paints—red, orange, yellow, green, blue, purple, and white
- paintbrushes
- plates or foam trays
- access to a sink or washing station
- paper towels
- page 73, reproduced for each child

Step by Step

1. Give children the tempera paints, paintbrushes, and trays.

2. Have children put a small puddle of red paint on the tray. Then have them paint the circle marked "red" on page 73.

3. Next, have children add one drop of white paint to the red puddle on the tray and mix it. Tell children to use the new color to paint the first circle in the "Add one drop of white." column.

4. Guide children to continue following the directions at the top of each column to mix colors and paint circles. Remind children to rinse the paintbrush before beginning a new row of colors.

Name _____

Mixing Colors with White

Colors of the color wheel	Add one drop of white. 💧	Add another drop of white. 💧💧	Add another drop of white. 💧💧💧
red	◯	◯	◯
orange	◯	◯	◯
yellow	◯	◯	◯
green	◯	◯	◯
blue	◯	◯	◯
purple	◯	◯	◯

Value

Shading Shapes

Children discover that shading adds dimension to shapes.

Materials

- newsprint or other drawing paper
- pencils

Step by Step

Drawing 1 . . . .

1. Give children the paper and pencils.

2. Have them draw a ball. Tell them to pretend that the sun is in the top-left corner of the page and that it is shining down on the ball.

3. Next, have children shade the right side of the ball.

4. Finally, have them lay in a shadow on the ground.

Drawing 2 . . . .

1. Give children the paper and pencils.

2. Have them draw a box. Tell them to pretend that the sun is in the top-right corner of the page.

3. Then have children shade the left side of the box and lay in a shadow on the ground.

4. Next, have them make the box into a house. Then have them add shading to the dark side of the house.

5. Lastly, have children draw a ball or a tree in the yard. Ask them, "Which way will the shadow go?"

Value

Two Butterflies

Children cut out and paint a butterfly using one color plus white paint.

Step by Step

1. Give each child the paper, paints, paintbrushes, a tray, and a pencil.

2. Have children fold the white construction paper in half. Then have them draw an outline of one-half of a butterfly shape and cut it out.

3. Next, tell children to open the butterfly shape and use their pencils to lightly sketch a line along the outside border. Then have them pencil in various shapes in the center of the butterfly.

4. Now have children paint their butterfly using only one color of paint mixed with white to create different values of that color.

   - First, they paint the outside border with the solid color. It will have the darkest value.

   - Then they mix that color with a little white and paint some of the shapes in the center of the butterfly.

   - Have children continue adding white to the previous color and painting until they have a very muted shade of the original color.

5. After the butterflies dry, display them on a wall.

Materials

(for each child)

- white construction paper—12" x 18" (30.5 x 46 cm)

- acrylic paints in various colors, including white

- paintbrushes in several sizes

- plate or foam tray

- a pencil

Texture

Learning About

Texture

The world is full of a variety of textures. Children have first-hand experiences with many textures. They know about rough rocks and smooth marbles.

Texture

Awareness of Texture

Children investigate their world and describe what they see and touch and how it looks and feels.

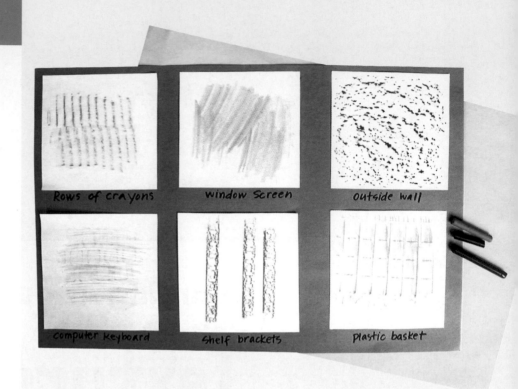

Materials

- newsprint or other drawing paper— 5" (13 cm) squares

- dark-colored crayons without paper wrappers

- large piece of colored butcher paper

- glue

Step by Step

1. Ask children to name words that describe how things look and feel. Write the words where children can see them. Sometimes it helps children to think in terms of opposites when compiling the list.

rough	grainy	hard
bumpy	prickly	fluffy

2. Give children the paper squares and crayons.

3. Then have them take the squares and crayons around the room and create rubbings of different textures.

4. Next, give children the butcher paper and have them mount each rubbing on it.

5. Lastly, have children label each texture as shown in the picture above.

HINT Challenge children to categorize their texture rubbings according to the descriptive words they listed.

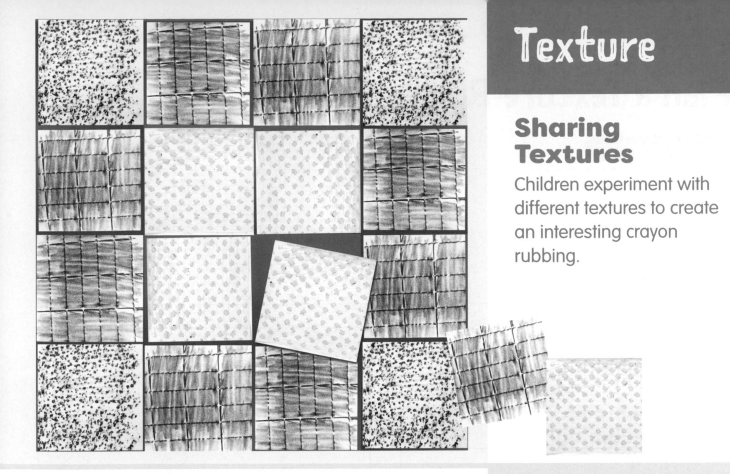

Texture

Sharing Textures

Children experiment with different textures to create an interesting crayon rubbing.

Step by Step

1. Explain to children that they will use crayons to create texture rubbings. Then give each child page 80, the crayons, and the construction paper squares.

2. Have children look at the crayon colors and page 80 to plan their color palette. Tell children to record their choices in the areas provided.

3. Have children follow the steps below to do rubbings:
   - Locate a textured surface.
   - Choose a crayon from the color palette they chose.
   - Make a rubbing on one of the small squares.

4. After children finish making the rubbings, give them the butcher paper and guide them to fold it into 16 squares.

5. Lastly, have children arrange the texture rubbings on the butcher paper, placing one rubbing in each square. Give children the glue. When they are happy with the design, have them glue the squares in place.

Materials

(for each child)

- colored butcher paper— 12" (30.5 cm) square

- white construction paper—eight 5" (13 cm) squares

- crayons with the paper wrappers removed

- glue

- page 80, reproduced for each child

- surfaces with interesting textures

Reproduce this page to use with Sharing Textures on page 79.

Name ______________________

Plan a Texture Rubbing

Color Palette

Primary Colors

____

____

____

Cool

____

____

____

Secondary Colors

____

____

____

Warm

____

____

____

Complementary Colors

____

____

____

Other

____

____

____

Textures

____

____

____

____

Now make your rubbings. Experiment with different patterns.
Then glue the squares in place in the pattern you like best.

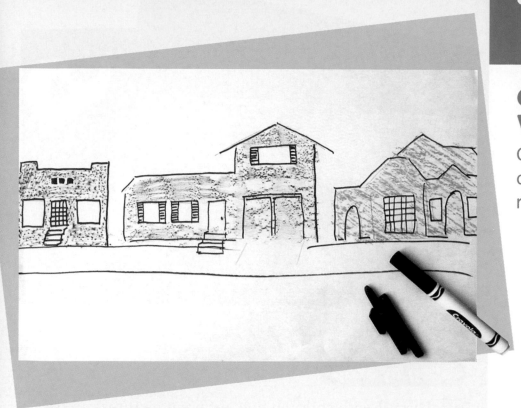

On the Street Where I Live

Children enhance a drawing with crayon rubbings.

Step by Step

1. Give each child the paper, crayons, pencil, and pen.

2. Then have children go outside and look at the houses along the street. Tell them they will be drawing those houses.

3. Next, have children do simple pencil drawings of several houses along a street. The houses should have areas large enough for children to do rubbings inside the lines.

4. After children finish drawing the houses, have them choose textures and do crayon rubbings to fill in the area of each building.

5. Lastly, have children outline the buildings and add details with the black crayon or felt-tip pen.

 HINT Have children create crayon rubbings to fill each section of an accordion-folded fan.

Materials

(for each child)

- white construction paper—12" x 18" (30.5 x 46 cm)

- crayons

- a pencil

- black crayon or felt-tip pen

Texture

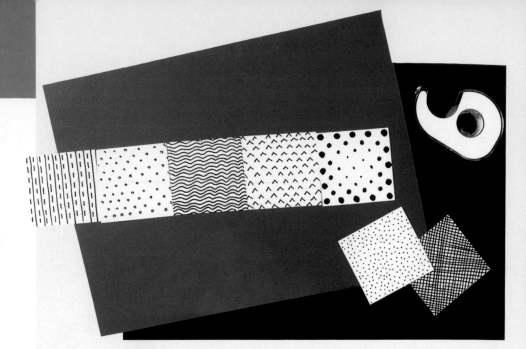

Repetition Creates Texture

Texture can be created in pictures by using repetition of lines and shapes. This repetition creates a rhythm that holds the pattern together.

Materials

- white construction paper—3" (7.5 cm) squares
- black crayons
- transparent tape

Step by Step

1. Discuss with children how different textures can be created by repeating a pattern. (Show an example for each statement below.)
   - One shape repeated over and over fills an area and creates a patterned effect.
   - Wavy lines drawn close together create movement and texture.
   - Cross-hatching (adding intersecting sets of parallel lines) adds shading and texture.
   - The distance between squiggles causes a change in the texture created.
   - Stippling (making tiny dots) can create texture.
   - Lines can be repeated in many variations. Lines and shapes repeated close together create a dark effect. Lines and shapes repeated farther apart create a lighter effect.

2. Give each child a 3" square of white construction paper. Have children use a black crayon to create a textured effect with a repeated line or shape.

3. Then lay all of the squares in a line and tape them together with transparent tape.

4. Display the line of squares and discuss the different textures created.

Creating Texture with Paint

Children investigate painting techniques that create textured effects.

Step by Step

1. Demonstrate some of the techniques that create texture in a painting.
   - thick, wavy paintbrush vs. narrow paintbrush
   - toothbrush rubbed across screen
   - overlaying or mixing colors
   - dry paintbrush
   - splatter
   - fingers
   - stipple (tiny dots)

2. Create a posterboard to display the techniques above. Then show children labeled examples of the techniques.

3. Lastly, give children paper, paints, paintbrushes, and assorted objects. Encourage them to experiment with different effects.

Materials

- easel paper
- tempera paints
- several different-sized paintbrushes
- assorted objects to use in creating textures: toothbrush, pencil, comb, plastic utensils, fingers, etc.
- posterboard

(HINT) Fingers can make quite a variety of textures. Patting, dragging, and scribbling with both the finger and the fingernail is very effective.

Texture

Textured Paint Collage

Children cut apart textured painted papers they have created and make new simple collage pictures.

Materials

(for each child)

- white construction paper—
  4" x 6" (10 x 15 cm)
  three 4" (10 cm) squares

- acrylic paints

- flat-ended paintbrush

- scraps of cardboard

- plastic fork, plastic knife, comb (any object that will help to create a texture)

- scissors

- glue

Step by Step

1. Give each child the construction paper, three paper squares, the paints, a paintbrush, scraps of cardboard, a plastic fork, scissors, and glue.

2. Squeeze a small amount of paint onto each square and allow children to experiment with creating different textures on each of their paper squares.

3. While the painted squares dry, brainstorm simple picture or design ideas that can be cut free-form from the squares.

4. Have children cut the shapes they brainstormed and glue them to the construction paper to make a collage.

How to Teach Art to Children • EMC 1016 • © Evan-Moor Corp.

Print a Texture

Sponges, potatoes, and gadgets are wonderful tools for printing texture and patterns in a picture.

Step by Step

1. Give children the paper, paints, sponges, potatoes, gadgets, and a tray.

2. Then have them fold their construction paper into fourths.

3. Follow the directions below to guide children to make a different print of their choice in each area of their paper.

4. Allow time for the paintings to dry and discuss the textured effects the children created.

> **How to Make a Print:**
> 1. Pour a puddle of paint onto a flat container.
> 2. Dip one edge of an object into the paint.
> 3. Press the painted edge on the paper.
> 4. Lift the object straight up.
> 5. Repeat dipping, pressing, and lifting.

Materials

- white construction paper—12" x 18" (30.5 x 46 cm)

- tempera paint in several colors

- sponges, potatoes, and gadgets (cookie cutters, forks, etc.)

- plates or foam trays

Texture

Scratch-Away Texture

Children create a scratchboard painting.

Materials

(for each child)

- white construction paper—9" x 12" (23 x 30.5 cm)
- crayons
- black tempera paint
- liquid detergent
- a paintbrush
- a plastic knife

Note: This is a messy procedure. Cover tables or desks with plastic or newspaper to make cleanup easier.

Step by Step

1 Give children the paper and crayons. Have children use the crayons to fill the paper with color (as shown below). The crayon lines should be thick and solid.

2 Mix the black paint with a few drops of the detergent. Give children the mixture and the paintbrushes. Tell them to paint over the completed crayon design with the mixture.

3 Allow the paint to dry completely.

4 Then guide children to carefully use the plastic knife to gently scratch the paint to create a picture or a design. As children "draw" with the knife, the color below the paint will be revealed.

A Collage Has Texture

A collage is a composition made by affixing pieces of paper, string, cloth, wallpaper, and other materials to a surface.

Step by Step

1. Have children choose one piece of construction paper as a background and one to create textured designs. Give them the copy paper, scissors, and glue.

2. Demonstrate several techniques for creating texture in a collage.

   - Tear the paper and leave a torn edge.
   - Cut the paper.
   - Crinkle the paper and then smooth it out.
   - Score the paper and bend it.
   - Twist the paper.
   - Pleat the paper.
   - Weave the paper in and out.
   - Layer the paper.

3. Then challenge children to use the other construction paper and the copy paper to create a collage. Encourage them to invent their own techniques to create texture.

4. Lastly, have children glue their textured pieces to the construction paper background.

Materials

(for each child)

- construction paper— two 9" x 12" (23 x 30.5 cm) sheets (one each of two colors)

- sheet of copy paper

- scissors

- glue

Texture

Texture a Tree

Groups of children cooperate in creating trees, incorporating various techniques to add texture to their projects.

Materials

- white butcher paper—36" (91.5 cm) squares
- assorted construction paper scraps
- assorted craft papers—paper bags, wallpaper, wrapping paper, tissue
- tempera paint in assorted colors
- paintbrushes, sponges, and gadgets
- scissors
- white glue

Step by Step

1. Set up a table with all the materials and space for children to complete the project.

2. Explain to children that they will create a tree using several different texture techniques. Then have children brainstorm different types of trees that they might create.

   - blossoming trees
   - fruit trees
   - evergreen trees with pine cones
   - oak tree with acorns
   - tree with fall-colored leaves

3. Next, have children plan their trees, making sure they understand they will use butcher paper to create the tree shape and the other materials to create colors and textures.

4. Then have children gather their materials and create their trees.

5. After children finish their trees, display them and encourage children to talk about what they did to create texture.

My Personal Collage

Children practice texture techniques to create a collage in an art center.

Step by Step

1. Set up a table with all the materials and space for children to complete the project.

2. Review texture techniques with children. Remind them that they can tear and cut paper, overlap patterns, use paint plus torn paper, and use special scissors.

3. Have children use the materials to build a collage.

4. Plan a time for children to share their collages and explain any special texture technique they developed.

(HINT) You can narrow the parameters of this experience by giving a specific topic.

- **Create a collage that represents Presidents' Day.**
- **Create a collage that shows your favorite pet.**

Materials

- 9" (23 cm) squares of cardboard for each student
- paper bags
- aluminum foil
- wallpaper scraps
- wrapping paper scraps
- colored papers
- packaging materials
- corrugated paper
- yarn
- cellophane
- tissue paper
- fabric
- egg cartons
- tempera paint
- paintbrushes
- scissors and pinking shears

Texture

Animal Collage

Children create two animals in a collage. The animals are the same, except one is a cut-paper design, and the other is a torn-paper design.

Materials

- newsprint or other drawing paper
- construction paper—

  white 12" x 18" (30.5 x 46 cm)

  scraps in assorted sizes and colors
- wallpaper, wrapping paper, paper bags, etc.
- crayons and felt-tip pens
- scissors
- white glue
- *Alexander and the Wind-up Mouse* by Leo Lionni

Step by Step

1. Read children the story of *Alexander and the Wind-up Mouse*. This fable serves as an example of cut versus torn-paper art. The "real" mouse in the story is created with a torn-paper edge. The mechanical mouse is made with a cut-paper edge.

2. Explain to children that they will make a collage and give them the materials for the project. Then have them choose an animal for their collage.

3. Have children draw the animal on the newsprint, encouraging them to use simple, basic shapes. Then tell them to cut out the animal body parts and use them to trace the animal shapes onto the construction paper. Each shape must be traced twice.

4. Children glue the cut-out animal body parts onto one of the traced shapes. Then they tear out another set of animal body parts and glue them onto the traced shapes.

5. Children may wish to create a background for their picture, using paper and pens to add details.

Cloth Collage

The different patterns and textures of cloth give children the opportunity to create varied and interesting collages.

Step by Step

1. Set up a table with all the materials and space for children to complete the project.

2. Explain to children that they will make a cloth collage. Show them an example of a completed project. Then children choose their cloth. Encourage them to use a variety of fabrics with different colors and designs.

3. Have each child get a piece of cardboard and experiment with different arrangements of cloth. They may want to try tearing as well as cutting the cloth to create pieces of an appropriate size. Patterns may overlap or weave in and out.

4. After they arrange their fabrics into a design that they are happy with, have them use a paintbrush to appy diluted white glue to the back of each fabric piece and press it onto the cardboard.

Materials

- cloth scraps (as many colors, textures, and patterns as possible)

- 8" (20 cm) squares of cardboard

- scissors that will cut cloth

- paintbrushes

- bowls of diluted white glue

HINT Cloth is hard to cut with classroom scissors. You may want to provide precut strips, squares, and circles.

Texture

Sandpaper and Paint Collage

Children build in different textures by beginning their design with pieces of sandpaper.

Materials

- sandpaper—3" (7.5 cm) squares of different textures
- construction paper for each child—6" x 9" (15 x 23 cm)
- tempera paint in several colors
- sponges, paintbrushes, and gadgets
- black marking pens
- glue

Step by Step

1. Explain to children that they will use sandpaper and paint to make a picture. Have them think about what they want the picture to look like.

2. Then give children the paper, paint, sponges, paintbrushes, gadgets, pens, and glue. Next, have them choose the sandpaper they will use.

3. Tell children that they may glue the sandpaper to the paper in the shape it has, or cut the sandpaper into a different shape and then glue it to the paper.

4. Next, have children use paintbrushes, sponges, or printing gadgets to add paint to the picture.

5. Allow the pictures to dry. Then invite children to add final details with a black marking pen.

How to Teach Art to Children • EMC 1016 • © Evan-Moor Corp.

Shape Rubbings

Children experiment with texture and color as they create this rubbing using one single shape.

Step by Step

1. Give children the paper, crayons, tape, and a variety of shape templates such as stars, hearts, ovals, squares, etc.

2. Have children tape a template of their choice to the tabletop.

3. Next, have them place the white paper over the template and use the side of a crayon to rub the paper. Soon, they will see the outline of the colored shape appear.

4. Have children move the template shape to a different place under the paper and repeat the process with a different color crayon. Encourage children to continue this process until they are happy with the result.

Materials

- white drawing paper— 9" x 12" (23 x 30.5 cm)
- crayons with the paper wrappers removed
- shape templates cut from old file folders or tagboard
- two-sided tape

Form

Learning About

Form

When a flat, two-dimensional shape is bent, a third dimension is created. The shape becomes a form. Artists use form when they create sculptures.

Some commonly used forms are cylinders, cones, spheres, cubes, pyramids, and prisms.

Form

What Is Form?

Children investigate how form is created. They discuss the difference between two-dimensional and three-dimensional objects.

Materials

- three-dimensional objects: soup can, ball, box, prism, cardboard paper roll, etc.
- 4 1/4" x 11" (10.8 x 28 cm) piece of paper for each child
- tape

Step by Step

1. Show children the can, ball, box, and prism. Explain that each is a form because it has three dimensions.

2. Then give children the paper and have them lay it flat on a table. Ask them if it is a form. The answer is *no* because it is flat.

3. Then have children roll the paper into a cylinder and ask the same question. Now the answer is *yes* because you have added a dimension and made it three-dimensional.

4. Lastly, give each child a piece of paper and two pieces of tape. Challenge them to create a form out of the paper. If the children choose to, they may cut or tear their papers as they create their forms.

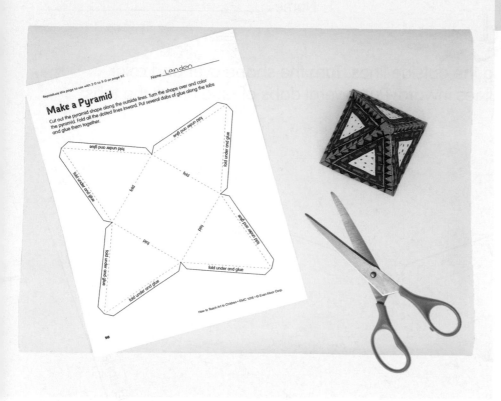

Children change a two-dimensional shape into a three-dimensional form.

Step by Step

① Give each child page 98, scissors, glue, and marking pens.

② Have children color the two-dimensional design and cut it out.

③ Next, have them fold the pattern on the fold lines.

④ After children fold the paper, have them put a dab of glue on each tab and create the pyramid.

⑤ Then discuss with children the difference between the two-dimensional shape and the three-dimensional form.

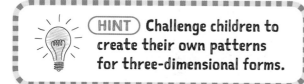

HINT Challenge children to create their own patterns for three-dimensional forms.

Materials

- scissors
- glue
- marking pens
- page 98, reproduced for each child

Name _____

Make a Pyramid

Cut out the pyramid shape along the outside lines. Turn the shape over and color the pyramid. Fold all the dotted lines inward. Put several dabs of glue along the tabs and glue them together.

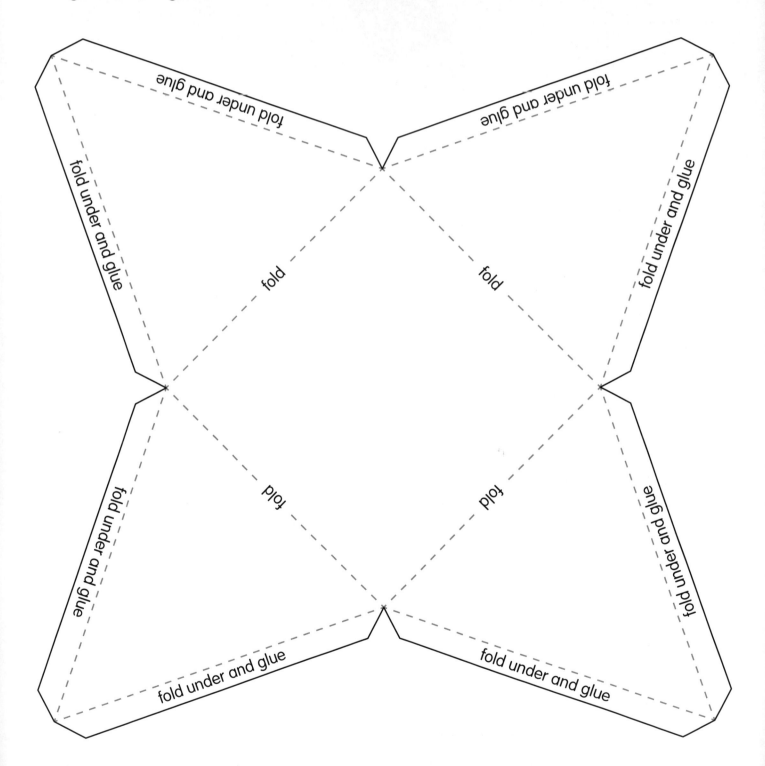

Form

Making a Form

Children practice making forms out of modeling clay.

Step by Step

1. Give each child a lump of clay. Show them how to work with it and share any rules they need to follow.

   For example:
   - *Clay stays on the work surface.*
   - *Put the clay back into its container when you are finished.*
   - *Clay is for modeling, not throwing.*

2. Guide children to practice modeling basic forms: spheres, pyramids, boxes, cylinders, etc.

3. After a child has a completed form, place it on a paper towel and label it with the child's name. You may choose to air dry it or fire it, or simply put it back into the clay container at the end of the project.

 (HINT) Try having children name each of the forms with a descriptive phrase.

a no-corner, smooth-all-over ball

Materials

(for each child)

- a fist-sized lump of clay
- flat surface for shaping clay
- paper towels

Form

Pinch a Pot

One basic form that artists make is a bowl. Using a simple pinch technique, children will make their own bowls.

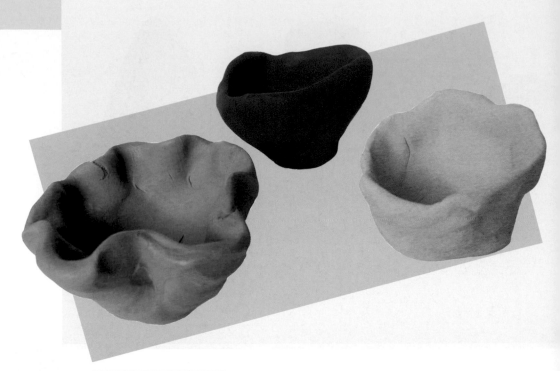

Materials

(for each child)

- 2" (5 cm) ball of clay
- flat surface for work

Baker's Clay:
- *1 cup (290 g) salt*
- *1 ½ cups (360 mL) warm water*
- *4 cups (500 g) flour*

1. *Mix salt and water.*
2. *Add flour.*
3. *Stir until combined.*
4. *Knead at least five minutes.*
5. *Store in an airtight container.*

Step by Step

1. Give each child a ball of clay. Explain that it is important to keep the clay in one piece as the form is pinched.

2. Have children stick their thumbs halfway into the clay balls.

3. With their thumbs still in the balls, children use their other four fingers to gently pinch the clay.

4. Next, have them gently turn the ball while pinching it so that an even rim is formed.

5. Dry or bake the clay.

HINT Use baker's clay to create the pinchpots. Bake the pots in the oven. Add colored accents with permanent markers and glaze the pots.

Stand 'Em Up

Children combine pairs of two-dimensional shapes into three-dimensional forms.

Step by Step

1. Give children the construction paper and scissors.

2. Then have them cut two small identical squares or rectangles from the construction paper. Shapes should not be larger than 5" (13 cm) tall.

3. Next, have children hold the two papers together and cut a slit halfway up.

4. Then guide children to reverse one of the shapes and slip one shape over the other to create a three-dimensional form.

5. Have children repeat the activity, making several forms in different sizes and colors.

Materials

- brightly colored construction paper
- scissors

Space

Learning About

Space

Space in artwork makes a flat image look like it has form. There are several ways an artist adds space to artwork:

- Overlapping—Placing an object in front of another object makes the object in front appear closer than the one behind.

- Changing Size—An object that is smaller looks like it is in the distance, while an object that is larger looks like it is closer.

- Using Perspective—Utilizing perspective, objects can be drawn on a flat surface to give an impression of their relative position and size.

Space

Overlapping Collage

Children use both overlapping and size in creating space.

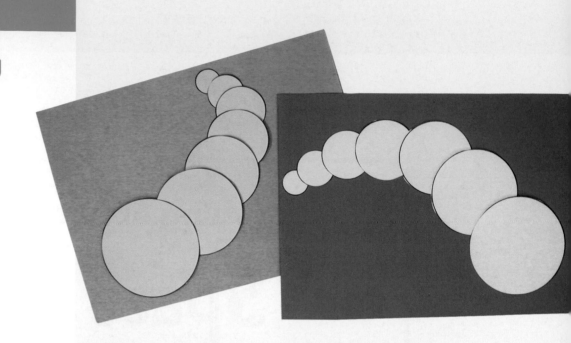

Materials

- page 105, reproduced on colored paper for each child
- construction paper— 9" x 12" (23 x 30.5 cm), assorted colors
- scissors
- glue

Step by Step

1. Give children page 105, the construction paper, scissors, and glue.

2. Have children cut out the different-sized circles on page 105.

3. Then have children choose a contrasting color for the background and arrange their circles on the background paper. Demonstrate how to use overlapping and size to create the illusion that a ball is coming toward the viewer.

4. Guide a discussion about the techniques children used to create the illusion. For example:

   - The smallest circle should be the farthest away and in back.

   - The next-smallest circle will overlap a small part of the previous circle.

5. After the discussion, children may wish to rearrange their circles. Once they are satisfied with their illusion, have them glue the circles in place.

Reproduce this page on colored paper to use with Overlapping Collage on page 104.

Space

Perspective, One-Point!

Perspective is a tool artists use to create space in their artwork. This time children will experiment with one-point perspective.

Materials

(for each child)

- 8 1/2" x 11" (21.5 x 28 cm) sheet of drawing paper
- a ruler
- a pencil
- an eraser

Note: This activity is intended for children age 11 or older.

Step by Step

1. Give each child a sheet of paper, a ruler, a pencil, and an eraser.

2. Guide children to trace a horizontal line parallel to the top and bottom of the paper as shown in the picture above. Then have them draw a dot on the horizon line. This is the **vanishing point**.

3. Next, have children draw a shape with corners anywhere on the paper.

4. Then have them use the ruler to draw lines to connect the corners of the shape to the vanishing point. If a line has to go across the shape to get to the vanishing point, children do not draw it.

5. Next, have children draw the backside of the shape parallel to the front of the shape.

6. Have children erase the lines beyond the shape that connect to the vanishing point.

7. Lastly, encourage children to shade their shapes in different values of color.

A Sunny Day

Children layer cutouts to show which object is closest.

Step by Step

1. Give children the colored rectangles and scissors. Have children cut the following shapes from the rectangles:

   - yellow—sun
   - green—top of a tree
   - red—house
   - blue—stairs

2. Next, have children layer the cutouts on the black paper. The farthest away should be in the back.

3. Then have children use the colored paper scraps from the rectangles to add details to the cutout.

4. Lastly, after children are happy with their pictures, have them glue all the pieces in place.

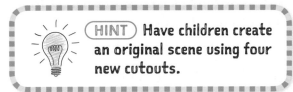

HINT Have children create an original scene using four new cutouts.

Materials

(for each child)

- construction paper—

  black 6" x 12" (15 x 30.5 cm)

  4" x 6" (10 x 15 cm)— one each: yellow, green, red, and blue

- scissors

- glue

A City in Perspective

Children use one-point perspective to create a cityscape that looks 3-D.

Materials

(for each child)

- white construction paper—12" x 18" (30.5 x 46 cm)
- a ruler
- a pencil
- an eraser
- colored markers
- black marker

Note: *This activity is intended for children age 11 or older.*

Step by Step

1. Give each child the paper, a ruler, a pencil, an eraser, and colored markers.

2. Have children draw a horizontal line about 2" (5 cm) from the bottom of the paper. Then, along the line, have them draw at least five different rectangles for building fronts.

3. Now tell children to draw a vanishing point on the top edge of the paper.

4. Next, have them connect the corners of the buildings to the vanishing point. If a line has to go through a building to get to the vanishing point, children do not draw it.

5. Tell children to draw the backs and sides of the buildings by drawing lines that are parallel to the front lines. Then have children erase the extra lines that continue to the vanishing point.

6. Invite children to add details such as windows, doors, signs, shingles, chimneys, antennas, etc.

7. Lastly, have them trace the pencil lines with black marker and use colored markers on the buildings.

Creativity takes courage.

—Henri Matisse

Where the spirit does not work with the hand, there is no art.

—Leonardo da Vinci

Art is not what you see, but what you make others see.

—Edgar Degas

I found I could say things with color and shapes that I couldn't say any other way—things I had no words for.

—Georgia O'Keeffe

Part Two

Contents

How to Teach Art to Children • EMC 1016 • © Evan-Moor Corp.

Using the Elements of Art

Artists use the seven elements of art in different ways in their art. Part Two of this book focuses on 23 famous artists, cultures, and types of art. An accompanying activity allows children to experience the style of each artist.

How to Use Part Two

The following art experiences help children see how artists from ancient times to the present have used the basic elements of art to express themselves.

The Art Experiences are based on the works of famous artists or types of art and include the following components:

- a brief background statement about the artist or type of art
- a list of the art elements that are the focal point of the experience
- references for learning more about the artist or art form
- a list of materials needed
- step-by-step directions for the experience

Step-by-Step Directions simplify the process of leading children through the art experiences. Follow these steps to use the experiences:

- Choose the experiences you want to use. The simplest ones are presented first, but all can be adapted to the appropriate level for your children.
- Explain the experience to children. Encourage creativity.
- Allow time for the thoughtful completion of the experiences.
- Discuss children's experiences and how they might parallel those of the famous artist or art form.
- Display finished art.

Twittering Machines

Paul Klee

Paul Klee was a Swiss-German painter who lived from 1879 to 1940. He loved music and played the violin. He was interested in creating deep meaning in his art by using symbols. He was very imaginative in his art. His work called *Twittering Machine* hangs in The Museum of Modern Art in New York. This work is a pen-and-ink drawing with watercolor. It depicts an imaginary machine that looks like it may make music when the handle is turned.

Read More About the Artist:

The Cat and the Bird: A Children's Book Inspired by Paul Klee by Géraldine Elschner

Dreaming Pictures: Paul Klee (Adventures in Art) by Paul Klee and Jürgen von Schemm

Paul Klee (Getting to Know the World's Greatest Artists) by Mike Venezia

Paul Klee (The Life and Work of) by Sean Connolly

Paul Klee: *Twittering Machine*

Talk About...

Show the children Paul Klee's *Twittering Machine*. Talk with children about Paul Klee and his love for music. Ask:

- What kind of music do you think the twittering machine plays?
- If you could create your own twittering machine, what kinds of sounds might it make?
- What would it look like?
- What kinds of colors did Paul Klee use in this work of art?

Materials

- print Paul Klee's ***Twittering Machine,*** page 2 in *Art and Artists* PDF

For each child:

- white construction paper— 12" x 18" (30.5 x 46 cm)
- black crayon
- watercolor paints
- water containers
- paintbrushes

Step by Step

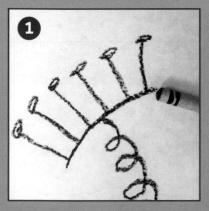

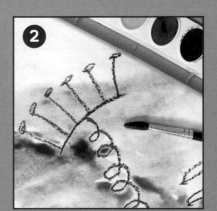

1 Give each child the paper and the black crayon. Challenge children to design their own twittering machines. Tell them to start by using lines and shapes to draw their machines. Next, have them add details.

2 Then give children the paint supplies and have them use the paintbrushes and water to wet the entire paper. Then have them drip cool colors onto the wet paper. The drops will spread out on the wet paper and blend together. Allow the paintings to dry.

3 Lastly, have children add a bit of a warm color to the inside of some of the shapes. After the paintings dry, have children sign and display their artwork.

Piet Mondrian

Piet Mondrian was born in 1872 and lived until 1944. He worked to create his own simple style of painting, and in the early 1900s his very modern style evolved. Mondrian used only straight vertical and horizontal lines and the three primary colors (red, yellow, and blue) with black and white.

Read More About the Artist:

Coppernickel Goes Mondrian by Wouter van Reek

Piet Mondrian by Hans Ludwig C. Jaffe

Piet Mondrian 1872–1944: Structures in Space by Susanne Deicher

Piet Mondrian: *Composition C (No. III) with Red, Yellow and Blue*

Talk About...

Show the example of Piet Mondrian's artwork and ask the children to describe it. Ask:

- What colors do you see?
- What kinds of lines do you see? How are the lines placed?
- What shapes do you see? Is this a picture of something you recognize?

Materials

- print Piet Mondrian's artwork, page 3 in *Art and Artists* PDF

For each child:

- thick string
- drying rack
- piece of cardboard—8" x 10" (20 x 25.5 cm)
- white construction paper—8" x 10" (20 x 25.5 cm)
- red, yellow, and blue crayons
- scissors
- masking tape
- black paint
- paintbrush

Step by Step

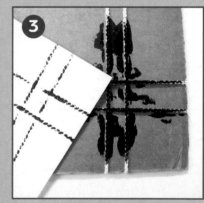

1. Give each child a piece of cardboard, paper, several yards of string, and several pieces of tape. Have children wrap a total of five pieces of string around the cardboard, both vertically and horizontally. Then have them cut the string and tape the ends on the back to keep the string tightly in place. This becomes a printing plate.

2. Next, have children paint the string with black paint. This process is called *inking the printing plate*.

3. Then have children position the printing plate paint-side down above the white paper and press it down to print the image of the black lines onto the paper. Have them lift it straight up and place the prints on a drying rack to dry.

4. Look again at Piet Mondrian's artwork. Ask the children to notice if every shape is colored. Ask if all the colored shapes are right next to each other or are spread apart. Then, using the crayons, have children color in three shapes with yellow, two with red, and four with blue. The colored shapes should be spread out just like in Mondrian's paintings.

Sunflowers

Vincent van Gogh

Vincent van Gogh (1853–1890) is famous for his use of raw color and wild brushstrokes. He became a painter after failing at many other careers. He painted day and night. He would set up still life arrangements to paint indoors when he couldn't paint outside. He painted his food, his shoes, and sunflowers in vases. His sunflowers are fun to look at, with their wild, bright yellow petals and their large dark centers. The vase he placed them in was also bright yellow.

Read More About the Artist:

van Gogh and the Sunflowers by Laurence Anholt

Camille and the Sunflowers: A Story About Vincent van Gogh by Laurence Anholt

The First Starry Night by Joan Shaddox Isom

Painting the Wind by Michelle Dionetti

van Gogh by Ingo F. Walther

Vincent van Gogh: *Still Life: Vase with Fourteen Sunflowers*

Talk About...

Show the example of Vincent van Gogh's *Sunflowers*. Ask:
- What colors did van Gogh use in the background?
- What about the sunflowers? The vase?
- Are the colors warm or cool?

Materials

- print Vincent van Gogh's artwork, page 4 in *Art and Artists* PDF

For each child:

- construction paper:

  background—blue 9" x 12" (23 x 30.5 cm)

  vase—yellow 6" x 9" (15 x 23 cm)

  stem—green 1" x 6" (2.5 x 15 cm)

  sunflower center—orange 3" (7.5 cm) square

- tissue paper—yellow, red, and orange, torn in strips

- chalk—light-colored and orange
- scissors
- glue
- toilet paper
- dried black beans

Step by Step

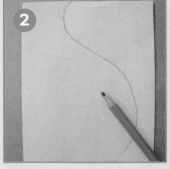 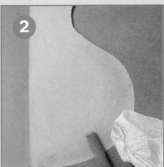  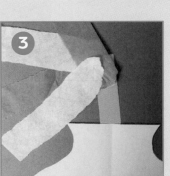

1 Give children the project materials. On the blue construction paper, have children draw a line one-fourth up from the bottom with light chalk and fill in the area below it. Use toilet paper to blend the chalk marks.

2 Next, have children cut out a vase shape from the yellow construction paper and lay it on their blue background. Then, using a piece of orange chalk, have them draw a line down the side of the vase. Tell them to rub the chalk line with toilet paper to create a shadow effect and the illusion of space.

3 Now have children place the green construction paper stem in the vase and arrange the tissue strips in a flower shape on the background paper.

4 Tell children to round the corners of the orange square to make the sunflower center. Then have them lay it on top of the tissue strips and glue the petals, stem, flower center, and vase in place.

5 Next, have children glue black beans onto the sunflower center. The beans add the texture.

Clay Cartouches

Ancient Egyptians

In ancient times, Egyptians used hieroglyphs to write messages in stone and on papyrus. The hieroglyphs (pictures and symbols) used by the Egyptians were their alphabet. By combining the pictures, the Egyptians could spell out words. On the walls of the pyramids, messages contain groups of hieroglyphs that are surrounded by an oval. These ovals with hieroglyphs in them are called cartouches. The hieroglyphs inside a cartouche spell a name.

Read More About the Art:

Ancient Egyptian Designs for Artists and Craftspeople by Eva Wilson

Egyptian Designs by Carol Belanger Grafton

Fun with Hieroglyphs by Catharine Roehrig

Hieroglyphs from A to Z: A Rhyming Book with Ancient Egyptian Stencils for Kids by Peter Der Manuelian

Pyramids: 50 Hands-on Activities to Experience Ancient Egypt by Avery Hart and Paul Mantell

Ancient Egyptian cartouche of Thutmose III, Karnak, Egypt

Talk About...

Show the example of the hieroglyphs on the cartouche on page 5 of the *Art and Artists* PDF. Relate the hieroglyphs to the alphabet. Explain that the cartouche spells the name of Thutmose III, an ancient Egyptian pharaoh.

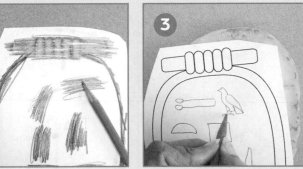

Materials

- print the cartouche containing hieroglyphs, page 5 in *Art and Artists* PDF

For each child:

- reproduce page 120, hieroglyphic alphabet
- reproduce page 121, oval cartouche pattern
- brown tempera paint
- paper towels
- clay
- paper clip
- paintbrush
- dull pencil

Step by Step

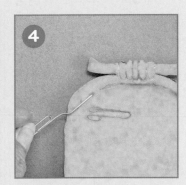

1 Give children the project materials. Have them place their oval cartouche pattern over the hieroglyphic alphabet paper and trace the characters that spell their name.

2 Then have them turn over the pattern and scribble with pencil on the backside. This creates a form of carbon paper so that when the pattern is placed on the clay, they can trace over the lines and transfer the symbols onto the clay.

3 Next, have children roll out a 1/4" (0.6 cm) thick layer of clay. Guide them to trace over the cartouche pattern and hieroglyphs with a dull pencil to transfer the design onto the clay.

4 Then have them use paper clips to cut away the extra clay along the outside of the cartouche pattern. Tell children to reinforce the pencil lines with the paper clip.

5 Allow the clay to dry and then fire it, bake it, or set up the clay as directed by the manufacturer.

6 Lastly, have children paint the entire cartouche with a thin layer of brown paint and then quickly wipe off the paint with a paper towel so that it remains only in the crevices.

Hieroglyphic Alphabet

Name _____

a	h	o	v
b	i	p	w
c	j	q	x
d	k	r	y
e	l	s	z
f	m	t	boy
g	n	u	girl

Cartouche Pattern

Name _____

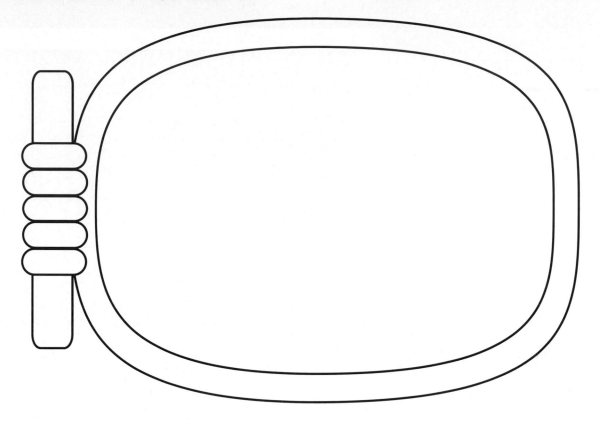

Cartouche Pattern

Name _____

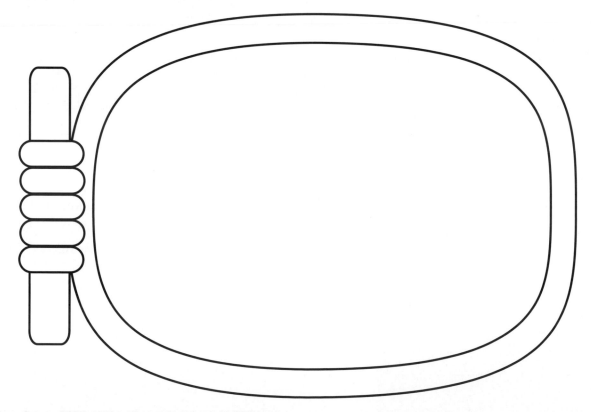

Adinkra Cloth

Adinkra Cloth

Adinkra cloth is made by the Ashanti peoples in Ghana, Africa. They use black ink to print symbols with different meanings on fabric. They make stamps out of gourds. Then they apply ink to the stamps and press them on the fabric. They may separate the squares of the designs with lines. The Ashanti often sew the pieces of cloth together with brightly colored thread to make clothes for special ceremonies.

Read More About the Art:

The Talking Cloth by Rhonda Mitchell

African Designs from Traditional Sources by Geoffrey Williams

Traditional African Designs by Gregory Mirow

West African Adinkra Symbols: 31 Rubber Stamps by Mimi Robinson

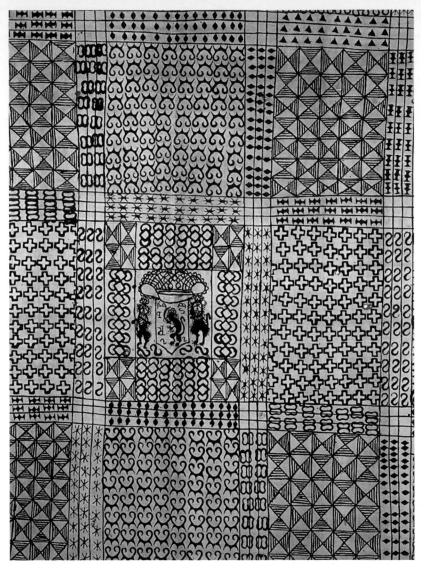

Adinkra cloth

Talk About...

Talk to the children about the Adinkra cloth and the Ashanti peoples. Point out where Ghana is on a map or globe. Ask the children if they notice anything in the Adinkra cloth (lines, shapes, repeated patterns).

Materials

- print the picture of the Adinkra cloth, page 6 in *Art and Artists* PDF

For each child:

- brown construction paper—9" (23 cm) square
- ruler
- black crayon
- gadgets to print with (objects that you have collected that will make an interesting image when inked and then stamped)
- black printing ink or tempera paint
- washable, portable flat surface or plate

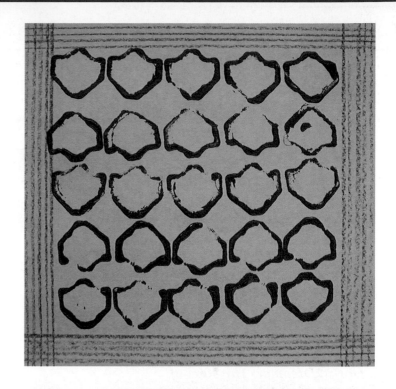

Step by Step

This project uses the design of an Adinkra cloth, substituting gadget prints for the elaborate stamps made by the Ashanti peoples.

1. Give children the project materials. Have children use the ruler and black crayon to make a border of straight lines around the construction paper square.

2. Next, have children choose a gadget and follow the steps below to print the same object in a repeating pattern on their square.

   - Pour a puddle of paint or ink on a flat surface or plate.

   - Spread the paint or ink into an even layer.
   - Place the gadget to be printed in the paint.
   - Press the paint edge of the gadget onto the paper.
   - Lift straight up.

3. After children finish printing the squares, allow the paint to dry completely. Children's squares may be combined to create a large Adinkra cloth.

Pop-up Collage Cards

Henri Matisse

Henri Matisse (1869–1954) painted large vibrant canvases in his early career. Later in his life, Matisse became ill and was confined to a wheelchair. Because he could no longer stand up at his canvases, he began to cut out paper designs and arrange them in attractive compositions. His *Jazz* series is very famous.

Read More About the Artist:

Colorful Dreamer: The Story of Artist Henri Matisse by Marjorie Blain Parker

The Iridescence of Birds: A Book About Henri Matisse by Patricia MacLachlan

A Bird or Two: A Story About Henri Matisse by Bijou Le Tord

Matisse (Famous Artists) by Antony Mason, Andrew S. Hughes, and Jen Green

Henri Matisse: *La Négresse*

Talk About...

Talk about Matisse's cutouts and the reason he began doing cutouts rather than paintings. Have children note the shapes in the collage. Also ask children to notice the colors that Matisse used.

card opened

card closed

Materials

- print Henri Matisse's paper collage, page 7 in *Art and Artists* PDF

For each child:

- construction paper— white 9" x 12" (23 x 30.5 cm) scraps in various colors
- scissors
- glue

Step by Step

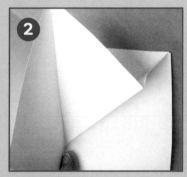

1 Give children the project materials.

2 Have children fold their white paper to make a pop-up card.

 a. Fold the paper in half lengthwise.

 b. Fold the top corner (fold side) down to the open edge.

 c. Turn the paper over and reverse the fold.

 d. Open the paper.

 e. Pull the top-center fold inside and to the left side of the page. Press folds firmly.

 f. Open the paper again.

 g. Fold the bottom to meet the top. Press fold firmly.

 h. Close the card so that the plain side is outside and the triangle fold is inside. Press firmly again.

3 Next, have children choose three colors of paper scraps to cut out shapes. After children cut out the shapes, have them arrange the shapes on the inside and outside of their cards.

4 After the shapes are arranged, use dots of glue to glue the shapes to the card. Allow the glue to dry.

Drawing an Invention

Leonardo da Vinci

Leonardo da Vinci (1452–1519) is a well-known artist and inventor. He was born in Italy in 1452. Leonardo da Vinci was known as a "Renaissance Man." He loved learning. He not only painted one of the world's most famous portraits, *Mona Lisa*, but he also made many contributions to science. He was an inventor, too. Leonardo da Vinci's drawings included ideas for many different inventions. He was always thinking. He even wrote backwards to keep people from stealing his ideas!

Read More About the Artist:

Who Was Leonardo da Vinci?
by Roberta Edwards

Leonardo and the Flying Boy
by Laurence Anholt

Da Vinci (Getting to Know the World's Greatest Artists)
by Mike Venezia

Da Vinci: The Painter Who Spoke with Birds (Art for Children)
by Yves Pinguilly

Leonardo da Vinci by Diane Stanley

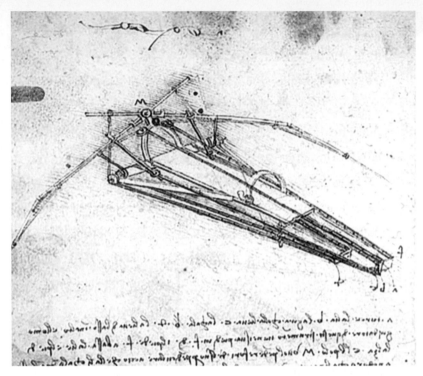

Leonardo da Vinci: Designs for a Flying Machine

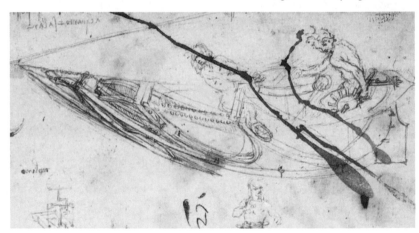

Leonardo da Vinci: Designs for a Flying Machine

Talk About...

Have the children look at examples of Leonardo da Vinci's drawings. Ask them what they think the different machines might do. Does it look as if Leonardo da Vinci took time to draw these inventions, or did he just scribble them out? Have children think about what invention they would make to help them in their lives.

Materials

- print Leonardo da Vinci's invention drawings, page 8 in *Art and Artists* PDF

For each child:

- white drawing paper
- manila paper—
  9" x 12" (23 x 30.5 cm)
- brown marking pen
- brown butcher or
  construction paper
- a pencil
- an eraser
- a ruler

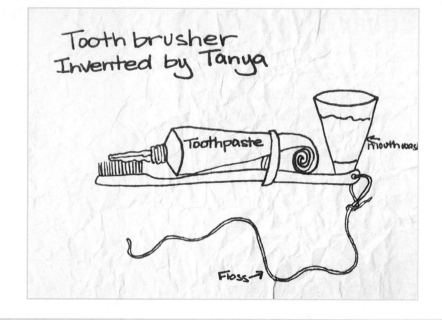

Step by Step

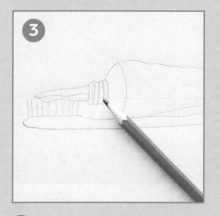

1 Tell children to imagine that they are inventors like Leonardo da Vinci. Ask them to draw a machine that will help them do something.

2 Give children the project materials. Have them draw three different ideas on the white drawing paper. Then help children choose one of their drawings or suggest that they combine several of their ideas into one machine.

3 After children have chosen their machines, have them draw their machines in pencil on the manila paper. They may add written instructions on their paper, as well.

4 Next, have children trace over their pencil lines with brown marker.

5 Then have children add texture to their paper by crumpling it and uncrumpling it several times to make it look old.

6 Lastly, have them mount the drawings on brown paper and display their creative ideas.

Edgar Degas

Edgar Degas (1834–1917) is famous for his paintings of ballerinas. He painted with Claude Monet during the Impressionist movement. However, Degas did not use short brushstrokes like Monet. Degas preferred to use a more realistic style. The dancers in Degas' paintings look like they might have been photographed. Degas was able to capture a single moment in his paintings and save it for many people to look at.

Read More About the Artist:

Edgar Degas: Paintings That Dance by Maryann Cocca-Leffler

Junior Edgar Degas: His Life and Art by Fiona Holt

Degas and the Little Dancer: A Story About Edgar Degas by Laurence Anholt

Edgar Degas (Getting to Know the World's Greatest Artists) by Mike Venezia

Edgar Degas: *The Dance Class*

Talk About...

Show the picture of Degas' ballerinas. Ask children to describe details about the dancers. Ask them if they have ever seen a ballerina.

Materials

- print Edgar Degas' ballerinas, page 9 in *Art and Artists* PDF
- print the solo ballerina picture, page 10 in *Art and Artists* PDF

For each child:

- white paper—12" x 18" (30.5 x 46 cm)
- thin black marking pen
- tempera paints—brown, green, blue, and purple
- a pencil
- an eraser
- oil pastels
- paintbrushes

Step by Step

1. Display the picture of the solo ballerina and give children the project materials.

2. Then have children look at the picture and draw the model quickly in pencil. Have them use light pressure on the paper so they can erase if they need to.

3. Next, have children add details to the dancer and the scene. For example, they may wish to add a stage to the background.

4. Then have children carefully trace over all lines with a black marking pen and paint the stage brown, leaving the ballerina unpainted.

5. Tell children to choose a cool color such as green, blue, or purple to paint the background wall. Remind them to be careful not to paint over the ballerina. Allow the paint to dry.

6. Lastly, show the children how to use oil pastels and have them color in their ballerinas with oil pastels. Use a skin color on the ballerina's skin and whatever color they choose for the costume, hair, and eyes.

Accordion Books

Chinese Bookmakers

Books with hard covers like those found in a library were first made in China.

- Before the invention of hard covers, long strips of paper were rolled into scrolls.
- These long strips of paper evolved into accordion books with hard covers.
- Later, the edges of the hard covers were sewn together on one side.

The Chinese also created a printing process that used carved blocks of wood to print images in books.

One strong symbol in the Chinese culture is the dragon. It stands for truth, life, power, nobility, and fortune. The dragon is often gold, green, or red, or a combination of all three colors.

Read More About the Art:

Behold...the Dragons! by Gail Gibbons

Mouse Match by Ed Young

A Chinese bamboo book

Talk About...

Discuss the history of bound books. Display the picture of the Chinese accordion book and talk about China and the invention of accordion books. Tell the children that they are going to make their very own accordion book.

Materials

- print the picture of the Chinese accordian book, page 11 in *Art and Artists* PDF

For each child:

- red tagboard—two 4" x 5" (10 x 13 cm) pieces
- white construction paper—4 3/4" x 15" (12 x 38 cm)
- stamp with different shapes made from foam material, mounted on a wooden block or jar lid
- 20" (51 cm) blue ribbon or yarn
- gold tempera paint
- glue
- a pencil
- crayons
- scissors
- flat surface or plate
- black marking pen

Step by Step

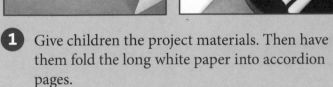

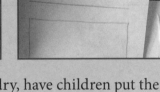

1 Give children the project materials. Then have them fold the long white paper into accordion pages.

- First, fold the paper in half.
- Next, fold the top end back to meet the fold and crease a new fold.
- Turn the paper over and do the same on the other side.

2 Next, have each child create a stamp by cutting foam material in a repeating design. Glue the pieces to a wooden block or jar lid.

3 Then have children press their stamps into the gold paint and print a pattern on their red tagboard covers. Allow the paint to dry.

4 After the paint is dry, have children put the books together.

- Lay the back cover with the decorated side touching the table.
- Lay the ribbon or yarn so the middle of it is in the middle of the back cover.
- Glue on the back end of the accordion-folded white paper and lay it down on the cover.
- Place a few drops of glue on the front end of the accordion pages and place the top cover on the book with the printed side facing out.

5 Encourage children use this book as a journal or as a sketch pad for their drawings.

Story Quilts

Faith Ringgold

Faith Ringgold is an important African-American artist. She was born in Harlem, New York, in 1930. Her artwork has a fun, imaginative quality. Most of her works are quilted paintings. She paints on canvas and then quilts a border to sew on the edges. Quilted paintings were photographed for the illustrations in her book *Tar Beach*. Faith Ringgold often includes herself and people she knows in her paintings.

Read More About the Artist:

Talking to Faith Ringgold by Faith Ringgold

Faith Ringgold (Getting to Know the World's Greatest Artists) by Mike Venezia

Faith Ringgold: *Tar Beach 2*

Talk About...

Read the book *Tar Beach* to the children and have them look at the illustrations. Explain to them that Faith Ringgold's paintings were quilts. Ask them to look for the lines where the paintings are sewn to the quilts. Also ask them to notice the quilted borders of her paintings. What kind of colors do they notice in the paintings?

Materials

- the book **Tar Beach** by Faith Ringgold
- print Faith Ringgold's *Tar Beach 2* quilt, page 12 in *Art and Artists* PDF

For each child:

- white construction paper—
  12" x 18" (30.5 x 46 cm)
- wrapping paper or wallpaper
  1 1/2" (4 cm) squares
- black marking pen
- crayons and colored
  chalk
- toilet paper
- a ruler
- glue
- a pencil
- an eraser

Step by Step

1. Give children the project materials. Then have them glue wallpaper or wrapping paper squares of contrasting colors around the edges of the white paper to create a "quilted" border.

2. Next, have children use a black marking pen to add little stitches around the squares to make it look like a quilt.

3. Then, in pencil, have them lightly draw a picture and write a story in the center of the paper. They may use a ruler to draw lines to keep their writing aligned.

4. Children use crayons to color their illustrations with a lot of bright colors like Faith Ringgold uses!

5. Next, have them trace over their story with marking pens.

6. Then, using a piece of chalk in a cool color (blue, green, or purple), have children lightly rub color into the background around the image and use toilet paper to blend in the color.

7. Lastly, have the children sign their quilts.

Still Lifes

Paul Cézanne

Paul Cézanne (1839–1906) was one of the leading artists at the end of the nineteenth century. He is well known for his paintings of landscapes and still lifes. Cézanne worked hard to use color and value to give his paintings depth. He believed that using contrasting tones and colors made his drawings and paintings successful.

Read More About the Artist:

Cézanne and the Apple Boy by Laurence Anholt

Paul Cézanne (Art Profiles for Kids) by Kathleen Tracy

Paul Cézanne (Getting to Know the World's Greatest Artists) by Mike Venezia

Paul Cézanne: *Still Life with Apples and Pears*

Talk About...

Discuss Paul Cézanne and his artwork with the children. Show his still life painting and ask children to tell what they think a still life is. Ask children to notice the values (lights and darks) in Cézanne's paintings.

Materials

- print Paul Cézanne's still life, page 13 in *Art and Artists* PDF
- white tablecloth, tall vase, and various fruits

For each child:

- construction paper—
  blue 11" x 17" (28 x 43 cm)
  white 6" x 17" (15 x 43 cm)
  gray 5" x 7" (13 x 18 cm)
  scraps of warm colors
- black and white chalk

- scissors
- glue
- toilet paper

Step by Step

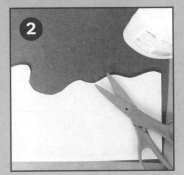
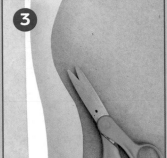
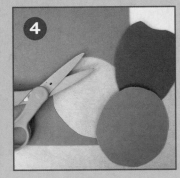

1 Set up a still life with a white tablecloth, a tall vase, and various fruits to serve as a model.

2 Give children the project materials. Have them follow the steps below to make the tablecloth.

- Using scissors, children cut one wavy edge in the white construction paper to represent the folds along the top of the tablecloth.
- Children glue the tablecloth to the blue background paper.

3 Next, have them cut out a vase from the gray paper. The vase may be cut on a folded sheet of paper so that it is symmetrical.

4 Then tell children to cut out colored fruit and arrange the vase and fruit on their tablecloths. By overlapping the shapes, they create space. After they are happy with their composition, have children glue their shapes in place.

5 Show children how to use the black chalk on one side of the shapes (vase and fruit) and the white chalk on the other side of the shapes to add form to the flat shapes. Explain that they are using value just like Cézanne did in his still life paintings. Blend the lines of chalk with toilet paper.

6 Tell children that they may also add blended chalk lines to create folds in the fabric of the tablecloth.

Pattern Portraits

Henri Matisse

Henri Matisse (1869–1954) was born in France. He studied to be a lawyer and then became an artist at the age of 23. Matisse used a lot of patterns in his paintings. In his travels he collected patterned fabrics from different places and looked at them as he painted. Matisse liked to paint with expressive lines and forms. His paintings are colorful and full of energy.

Read More About the Artist:

Henri's Scissors by Jeanette Winter

Henri Matisse: Drawing with Scissors by Jane O'Connor

Matisse: The King of Color by Laurence Anholt

A Bird or Two: A Story About Henri Matisse by Bijou Le Tord

Matisse (Famous Artists) by Antony Mason, Andrew S. Hughes, and Jen Green

Henri Matisse: *Still Life with Eggplant*

Talk About...

Talk about Matisse and his artwork. Have the children locate the patterns in the painting. Talk about Matisse's travels and how he collected fabrics to use in his paintings.

Materials

- print Henri Matisse's painting, page 14 in *Art and Artists* PDF
- clothing and fabric with patterns
- a vase with flowers
- a table
- a chair

For each child:

- white drawing paper— 11" x 17" (28 x 43 cm)
- black construction paper— 12" x 18" (30.5 x 46 cm)
- tempera paints— black and colors
- skin-tone oil pastels
- paintbrushes
- a pencil
- glue

Step by Step

1. Set up a live still life with a chair, patterned fabric on a table, a vase with flowers, and a model dressed in patterned clothes.

2. Give children the project materials and have them sketch the scene lightly in pencil on the white paper.

3. Then, using a thin brush and black paint, have children trace the pencil lines. Allow the paintings to dry.

4. Next, have children sketch a patterned background behind the model and paint the background and clothes in colorful patterns, leaving the skin uncolored. Allow the paintings to dry.

5. Lastly, have children fill in all skin areas with the skin-tone oil pastels.

6. Mount the paintings on black paper and display them for children to enjoy.

Musician Collages

Pablo Picasso

Pablo Picasso was born in Spain in 1881 and died in France in 1973. Picasso was always shocking people with his artwork. His painting style changed more over the period of his life than that of any other great artist. He helped invent a kind of art called Cubism. A lot of his paintings look like he has broken the object he was painting into blocks or cubes. He was also one of the first artists to use a collage technique by adding different objects to his paintings.

Read More About the Artist:

Picasso and the Girl with a Ponytail by Laurence Anholt

Picasso (Famous Children) by Tony Hart

Pablo Picasso (Getting to Know the World's Greatest Artists) by Mike Venezia

What's So Great About Picasso? A Guide to Pablo Picasso Just For Kids! by Max Tanner

Pablo Picasso: *Three Musicians*

Talk About...

Show children the picture of Picasso's *Three Musicians*. Ask them to find the three musicians and their instruments. Ask:

- What do you notice about the people?
- Are they realistic or stylized?
- What kinds of shapes do you see?

Materials

- print Pablo Picasso's *Three Musicians,* page 15 in *Art and Artists* PDF

For each child:

- scraps of wallpaper and wrapping paper
- construction paper—
  black 12" x 18" (30.5 x 46 cm)
  green 11" x 17" (28 x 43 cm)
  scraps of black, white, and assorted colors
- black permanent marking pen
- scraps of gold foil paper
- scissors
- glue

Step by Step

1. Give children the project materials. Then, using the scraps of paper, have children cut out shapes to make their musicians. They should give their musicians a hat like the musicians in the painting and use patterned paper for their clothes. Encourage children to use mostly squares and rectangles.

2. Next, have children arrange the shapes to create their musicians on the green paper. After they are happy with their layouts, have them glue the shapes in place.

3. Then have children choose the instrument their musician will play. Using the gold foil paper, have them cut out the instrument and glue it in place.

4. Tell children that they can add details with a permanent black marker.

5. Mount the pictures on black paper and display them for children to enjoy.

Black and White Pottery

Anasazi Peoples

The Anasazi peoples lived in the southwestern United States. They are remembered for their homes, which were built into cliffs. The Anasazi peoples are the ancestors of the Pueblo Indians, who now live in New Mexico. About AD 900, Anasazi artists began making their well-known black-and-white pottery. It has intricate geometric designs similar to the woven designs of their baskets. This pottery was formed using a coil technique. When the pottery was leather hard, it would be burnished with a smooth polishing stone. Once the pottery was polished, the geometric designs were painted on using a brush made out of yucca leaves. The "paint" was a bee-plant extract. The pottery was then pit-fired, which turned the painted areas black while the unpainted areas remained white.

Read More About the Art:

Anasazi by Leonard Everett Fisher

The Anasazi by David Petersen

Chaco Anasazi bowl

Chaco Anasazi ladle

Talk About...

Show children the pictures of the Anasazi pottery. Then talk about Anasazi culture and show pictures of their cliff dwellings. Have children look for the elements of art that are included in their pottery designs.

Materials

- print the pictures of black-and-white Anasazi pottery, page 16 in *Art and Artists* PDF
- kiln, oven, or place to dry the pots
- examples of designs from Anasazi pottery

For each child:

- white clay (Depending on your facilities, you may use real clay, oven-bake clay, or air-drying clay.)
- drawing paper
- black marking pen
- a pencil
- thin paintbrush
- black tempera paint

Step by Step

1 Give children the project materials. Then follow the steps below to have them form pinch pots.

- Have children use the clay to make a ball that is about the size of a golf ball.

- Then have them put the ball on the end of their thumb, being careful not to push the thumb through the clay. Tell them to begin pinching the ball between their thumb and other fingers. Have them rotate the ball as it is pinched until a bowl is formed.

2 Next, have children add coils to the pinch pot.

- Tell them to take a bit more clay and roll it into a 1/2"-wide (1.25 cm) coil.

- Then, attach the coil to the top rim of the pinch pot. (If you are using regular clay, children will need to slip and score both areas to stick them together.)

- Children blend in the coil to the top rim of the pot.

- They may add as many coils as they want.

- Tell children to write their names with a pencil on the bottom of their pots.

3 Allow the pots to dry according to the manufacturer's directions.

4 Talk to the children about the designs on Anasazi pottery. Show examples. Have children practice making some geometric designs with the black marker on the paper.

5 After the pots are dry, have children use thin brushes and black tempera paint to paint on their chosen design.

Tessellations

M.C. Escher

Maurits Cornelis Escher was born in the Netherlands in 1898 and died in 1972. His interest in tessellation developed after seeing a tile floor in Spain in 1936. He worked to animate the tessellating shapes instead of working with abstract geometrical designs. Escher incorporated his animated tessellation into his woodcuts and lithographs.

Read More About the Artist:

The M.C. Escher Coloring Book: 24 Images to Color by M.C. Escher

M.C. Escher: His Life and Complete Graphic Work by J.L. Locher

The M.C. Escher Sticker Book: 79 Imaginative Stickers by M.C. Escher

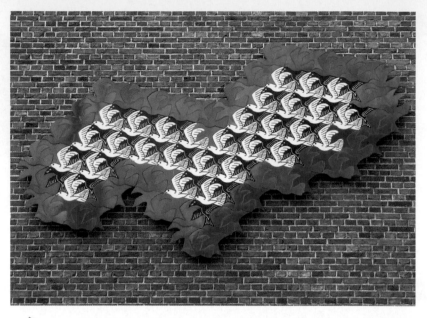

M.C. Escher: Wall tableau of a tessellation on the Princessehof Ceramics Museum, Leeuwarden, Netherlands

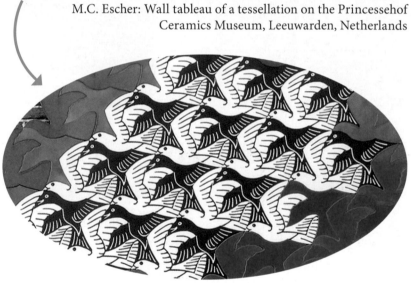

Talk About...

The word *tessellation* comes from *tessera*, which is a small stone or tile used in Roman mosaics. We can find tessellations everywhere around us in tile, wallpaper, and fabric designs.

Talk about M.C. Escher and his artwork. Discuss tessellations. Then look for examples of tessellation around the room.

Materials

- print M.C. Escher's *tessellation* image, page 17 in *Art and Artists* PDF

For each child:

- tagboard or thick paper— 3" (7.5 cm) square
- crayons and colored pencils
- white paper—9" x 12" (23 x 30.5 cm)
- black fine-point marking pen
- scissors
- tape
- a pencil
- practice paper

Step by Step

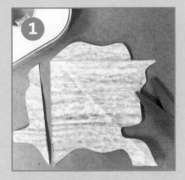 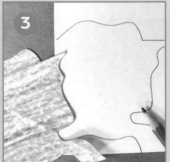  

1. Give children the project materials. Then follow the steps below to have them make a template shape from the tagboard square.

   - Have children use a crayon to color one side of the square. The other side is left uncolored. Use the colored side.

   - Starting at the upper-left corner and ending at the lower-left corner of the same side, have children cut an interesting line.

   - Then tell them to slide the cut piece straight across the square and tape it on the opposite side.

   - Using the same technique, have children cut a line from the bottom-left corner to the bottom-right corner.

   - Slide the piece straight up and tape it on the top of the square.

2. Ask children to decide what this shape will be. Then have them lightly pencil in defining lines on the template.

3. Next, have children trace the template onto the white paper. Tell them to place the template in the bottom-left corner of the white paper and carefully trace around it. Then have them move the template to the right and fit it into the edge of the first tracing. There should be no gaps. They will continue to trace and move the template until they fill the entire paper.

4. Now have children use a pencil to draw the details inside their shape. Children then carefully trace over their pencil lines with a black fine-point marking pen.

5. Lastly, have children use crayons or colored pencils to color their tessellation.

Pop Art Sculpture

Claes Oldenburg

Claes Oldenburg, born in 1929, is one of Pop Art's creative artists. Pop Art became popular during the late 1950s. Pop artists took familiar objects from society and made a statement about them by including these regular objects in their artwork. Oldenburg is well known for his larger-than-life sculptures of everyday objects. He made a giant hamburger that is six feet wide and a bag of shoestring potatoes that is nine feet tall. Oldenburg first makes a life-size model, sculpts the large object out of fabric, and then paints it. Other objects included in his sculptures are a telephone, scissors, ice bag, and a large spoon with a cherry on it. These ordinary objects became extraordinary sculptures.

Read More About the Artist:

The American Eye: Eleven Artists of the Twentieth Century by Jan Greenberg and Sandra Jordan

Claes Oldenburg, Coosje van Bruggen edited by Germano Celant

Printed Stuff: Prints, Posters, and Ephemera by Claes Oldenburg: A Catalogue Raisonne 1958–1996 by Richard H. Axsom

Claes Oldenburg and Coosje van Bruggen: *Flying Pins*, Eindhoven, the Netherlands

Claes Oldenburg and Coosje van Bruggen: *Cherry Sculpture*, Minneapolis, Minnesota

Talk About...

Show the pictures of Claes Oldenburg's sculptures and talk about Pop Art. Ask the children what objects they think a pop artist would choose to represent today. Have them look around the room to find an ordinary object they would like to make into a large sculpture.

Materials

- print Claes Oldenburg's sculptures, pages 18 and 19 in *Art and Artists* PDF

For each child:

- practice paper to sketch ideas
- boxes, balloons, paper tubes, and other objects to help create the basic form of the sculpture
- tagboard or cardboard
- newspaper torn in strips
- papier-mâché paste
- wire, aluminum foil, and string
- glue
- a pencil
- a marker
- tape
- a bowl
- scissors
- tempera paint
- paintbrushes

Step by Step

1. Give children the project materials. Then have each child choose an object and make a drawing of it.

2. Next, guide children to create the basic form of the object using boxes, balloons, tubes, and tape.

3. Have children cover their object with newspaper strips dipped in the papier-mâché paste. Allow time for the sculpture to dry completely.

4. Have children follow the steps below to paint their sculptures.

   - First paint the entire sculpture with the main color of their object.
   - Allow the paint to dry.
   - Then paint or use a marker to add any details.
   - Add any extra objects for detail.

5. Have children display their Pop Art sculptures.

Bark Paintings

Australian Aborigines

The Aborigine peoples of Australia created an art form called bark painting. Originally these paintings were not meant to be a work of art, but rather a form of communication. The paintings were created to tell stories. A distinctive quality of these bark paintings is the use of repetitive dots and circles. Pigments from natural sources like plants were painted on the bark of eucalyptus trees. The pigments were usually brown, white, tan, yellow, red, and black. Contemporary art from Australia includes acrylic paints instead of the natural pigments.

Read More About the Art:

Aboriginal Art of Australia: Exploring Cultural Traditions (Art Around the World) by Carol Finley

Dreamings: The Art of Aboriginal Australia by Peter Sutton

Bark paintings of kangaroo and rainbow serpent by Jimmy Njiminjuma, Aboriginal artist

Talk About...

Talk about Aboriginal bark paintings. Have children notice the use of lines and dots. Discuss what the paintings show and why children think the artists chose to paint those animals.

Materials

- print the Aboriginal bark paintings, page 20 in *Art and Artists* PDF

For each child:

- brown paper grocery bag
- blue construction paper—12" x 18" (30.5 x 46 cm)
- oil pastels—brown, white, tan, yellow, red, and black
- colored chalk

- a pencil
- scissors
- glue
- toilet paper

Step by Step

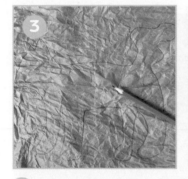 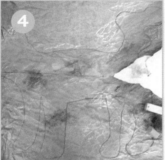 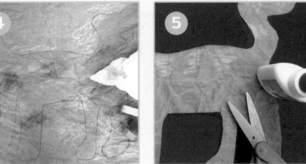 

1. Give children the project materials. Ask them to think about the animal they would like to have on their bark painting.

2. Have children cut out the front or back panel of a grocery bag and crumple and uncrumple it several times to make it look like bark.

3. Next, on the crumpled paper, have them draw a pencil outline (contour) of the animal they chose.

4. Then have them lightly rub their choice of chalk onto their animal to fill the entire shape. Tell children to use a piece of toilet paper to blend the chalk into the paper.

5. Next, have them cut out their animal along the lines of their pencil drawing and glue it in the center of the blue construction paper.

6. Encourage children to add details to their animals using oil pastels.

7. Talk about lines and circles. Have children think about how lines can symbolize feelings or characteristics such as loud, soft, nice, or mean. Ask them to decide what feeling they want to express about their animals. Then, using lines and circles that express that feeling, have them use oil pastels to create a design around the animal. For example, a picture of a grizzly bear might be surrounded by zigzag lines representing its growl. A snake might be surrounded by wavy lines representing the way it moves.

Mosaics

Roman Tile Workers

Mosaics are created by using different-colored tiles to make an image. The tiles are usually laid in a mortar to keep them in place. Mosaics were used by the Romans to decorate their cathedrals and churches. The tiles they used included bits of glass, stone, and gold. Often the subject matter focused on religious and political images, because that was what was important to the people of the Roman culture.

Read More About the Art:

Amazing Mosaics by Sarah Kelly

Geometric Patterns from Roman Mosaics by Robert Field

Mosaics of the Greek and Roman World by Katherine M.D. Dunbabin

Ancient Roman mosaic of a partridge perched on a branch, UNESCO golden mosaic floor of the Aquileia basilica

Abstract ceramic mosaic

Talk About...

Show children the pictures of mosaics. Ask them if they have seen any simple mosaics in their home (tile counters or showers). Tell them that the mosaics in our homes are much simpler than the mosaics created during the Roman Empire. The Romans used brilliant colors of glass to create their mosaics.

Materials

- print the mosaics, pages 21 and 22 in *Art and Artists* PDF

For each child:
- black construction paper— 9" x 12" (23 x 30.5 cm)
- paper scraps and magazine pages cut into small squares
- glue or glue stick
- a pencil

Step by Step

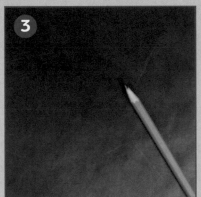  

1. Invite children to pick a topic for their mosaic. It can be an animal, a person, or a simple design.

2. Place the small cut paper squares on a table where children can access them. Then give children the other project materials.

3. Tell children to lightly sketch their chosen design on the black paper. Next, have children choose cut paper squares in the colors they want their mosaic to be.

4. Then have children arrange the paper squares on their black paper to create their image. Encourage them to leave a black border around each tile to represent the mortar that holds all the pieces together in a real mosaic. Children can use their knowledge of value and placement to create space in their pictures.

5. After children are happy with the way they laid out their images, have them glue the colored squares in place.

Flowers

Georgia O'Keeffe

Georgia O'Keeffe (1887–1986) is one of America's greatest painters. She was born in Wisconsin in 1887. At the age of twelve, Georgia's mother signed her up for painting lessons. Georgia decided to become an artist. She wanted to create art that was personal and expressed her feelings. Later on, Georgia moved to New York to go to art school. In 1924 she began to paint flowers. She painted them big and colorful so that the busy New Yorkers would stop and take time to look at them.

Read More About the Artist:

Through Georgia's Eyes by Rachel Victoria Rodriguez

My Name Is Georgia: A Portrait by Jeanette Winter

Georgia Rises: A Day in the Life of Georgia O'Keeffe by Kathryn Lasky

The Georgia O'Keeffe Museum by Peter H. Hassrick

Portrait of an Artist: A Biography of Georgia O'Keeffe by Laurie Lisle

Georgia O'Keeffe: *Petunias*

Talk About...

Show children Georgia O'Keeffe's flower painting. Ask them:
- Do O'Keeffe's flowers fill the page and touch the edges, or are they small and in the center of the page?
- Did O'Keeffe use one flower or many flowers?
- Do the flowers look real or abstract?
- How does she make the flowers look real?

Materials

- print Georgia O'Keeffe's painting, page 23 in *Art and Artists* PDF

For each child:

- print the pictures of flowers on pages 24 and 25 of the *Art and Artists* PDF
- white drawing paper— 18" x 24" (46 x 61 cm)
- a pencil
- colored chalk
- toilet paper
- spray fixative

Step by Step

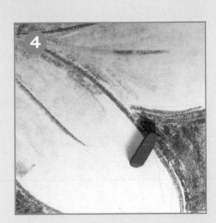

1. Give children the project materials. Have them look at the pictures of flowers and tell them to choose one flower they would like to paint in Georgia O'Keeffe's style.

2. Then have children use a pencil to very lightly draw one flower to fill the entire drawing paper. The drawing must touch all four sides of the paper. Point out to children that by drawing their flower, they are using line and shape.

3. Next, demonstrate how to use the colored chalk lightly in some areas and darker in other areas to create space in the flower. Inside the flower will be darker, while the outer areas of the petals that are in the light will be lighter. Then show children how to use a bit of the toilet paper to lightly blend the chalk. By using different values, children will create space in their drawings.

4. Have children use the colored chalk to add detail to their flowers.

5. After children finish their flowers, ask them what their flower's predominant color is. Then have them choose the complementary color from the color wheel and use that color to fill in the space around the flower.

6. After children complete their artwork, spray the drawings with spray fixative to set the chalk and then display the beautiful flowers.

Pop Art Food Posters

Andy Warhol and Roy Lichtenstein

In the 1950s, Pop Art became popular. Pop artists used items that were familiar and made a statement about them. Two of the most famous Pop artists were Andy Warhol and Roy Lichtenstein. Andy Warhol used a photo silk-screening process to put images from the media onto his large canvases. He is known for his repeated use of the same image. Some of his most famous works show Marilyn Monroe, Elvis Presley, Campbell's soup cans, and money. Roy Lichtenstein painted his images in the style of a comic strip. His paintings are made up of dots to imitate the "Benday" dots used to mass print images in books and papers.

Read More About the Artists:

Uncle Andy's: A Faabbbulous Visit with Andy Warhol by James Warhola

The Essential Andy Warhol by Ingrid Schaffner

Andy Warhol (Getting to Know the World's Greatest Artists) by Mike Venezia

Roy Lichtenstein's ABC by Bob Adelman

Roy Lichtenstein (Basic Series) by Janis Hendrickson

Andy Warhol design for the 1967 album *The Velvet Underground and Nico*

Roy Lichtenstein: *Still Life with Pitcher and Apple*

Talk About...

Show children the pictures of Andy Warhol's and Roy Lichtenstein's artwork. Ask them what images these artists might use if they were taking popular items from today's culture.

Talk about the dots in Lichtenstein's artwork. Have the children practice making dots with the tips of colored markers on a piece of practice paper. Notice that dots close together give a darker value than dots placed farther apart. When two colors of dots are mixed, the colors change.

Materials

- print Andy Warhol and Roy Lichtenstein's artwork, pages 26 and 27 in *Art and Artists* PDF

For each child:

- a pencil
- a ruler
- white construction paper— 9" x 12" (23 x 30.5 cm)
- marking pens—black permanent fine-tipped pen, assorted colors of watercolor pens

Step by Step

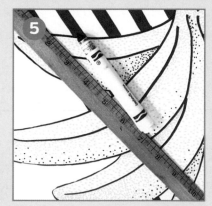

1. Give children the project materials. Then have each child think of a food item to draw.

2. Tell children to make a contour line drawing (outside line only, no fill or shading) of the food item they chose in pencil on the white paper. The food item should fill the page.

3. Next, have children trace over their pencil lines with fine-tipped black markers.

4. Then, using dots made with the tips of markers, have children add color to their drawings. Remind them that they must use dots! Explain to children that they can create value by using the dots close together or far apart and can mix dots to create different colors. They can also use dots in different ways to give their food texture.

5. Tell children to pick one or two colors that contrast with their food. Then, using a ruler, have them draw stripes to fill in the background.

6. Lastly, have children sign their artwork and display it!

Self-Portraits

Vincent van Gogh

Vincent van Gogh was not well known during his lifetime, but he is now known as one of the world's greatest artists. Vincent was a sad man and did not smile in his self-portraits, though he painted many of them. During his painting career, van Gogh sold one painting for $80. Today his paintings, which use thick paint and colors straight out of the tube, are worth millions. This thick or heavy use of paint showing the marks of the brush is known as impasto. Vincent van Gogh used impasto to add feelings and emotions to his paintings.

Read More About the Artist:

Vincent van Gogh: Sunflowers and Swirly Stars by Joan Holub

Vincent's Colors by Vincent van Gogh (Author), The Metropolitan Museum of Art (Contributor)

Camille and the Sunflowers: A Story About Vincent van Gogh by Laurence Anholt

The First Starry Night by Joan Shaddox Isom

Painting the Wind by Michelle Dionetti

Van Gogh (Basic Art) edited by Taschen

Vincent van Gogh: Self-Portrait

Talk About...

Show children Vincent van Gogh's self-portrait. Ask them to notice his use of thick paint and explain the term impasto. Ask children to notice van Gogh's expression, his position, and the texture created by the impasto.

Materials

- print Vincent van Gogh's self-portrait, page 28 in *Art and Artists* PDF

For each child:

- tagboard or thick paper—two 12" x 14" (30.5 x 35.5 cm) sheets
- black fine-tipped permanent marking pen
- thick tempera paint—Mix 1 tablespoon of cornstarch or flour with each 1/2 cup of paint. Paint colors are needed for skin tones, hair, eyes, lips, and clothing.
- torn bits of colored tissue paper

- white glue
- scissors
- a pencil
- a hand mirror
- a paintbrush
- foam egg carton

Step by Step

1 Give children the project materials. Have each child take his or her piece of the thick paper or tagboard, look in a mirror, and use a pencil to draw themselves from the shoulders up. Explain that their upper body should go off the bottom of the paper, and their heads should almost touch the top of the paper.

2 Then, using a paintbrush, have children apply thickened paint to their faces, eyes, lips, hair, and clothes to give them a more textured look. Allow the paint to dry.

3 Next, have them trace over the portrait lines with the black marking pen.

4 Now have children cut out their self-portrait.

5 Using watered-down glue and a brush, tell children to cover a second sheet of paper with torn tissue paper bits. The pieces should overlap one another. Suggest that they pick a color family (warm or cool) and keep their background colors in that family.

6 After the tissue paper is dry, have children glue their self-portrait onto the background.

7 Lastly, have them sign their artwork and display it.

Rock Art

Prehistoric Peoples

Humans have communicated in one way or another throughout history. One way we communicate is by writing symbols or drawing pictures. Rock art is an example of how prehistoric people communicated and recorded their lives. There are two different types of rock art. Pictographs are drawn or painted on the surface of the rock. Petroglyphs are carved into the rock.

Read More About the Art:

Native American Rock Art: Messages from the Past by Yvette La Pierre

Stories in Stone: Rock Art Pictures by Early Americans by Caroline Arnold

Pictograph: Archaeological prehistoric human cliff painting, over 4,000 years ago, Nakhon Ratchasima, Thailand

Petroglyph: A petroglyph of a caravan of bighorn sheep near Moab, Utah

Talk About...

Show children the pictures of rock art and invite them to make observations about what they see. Ask them if they can tell the difference between two different types of rock art. Talk about pictographs and petroglyphs. Also talk about the images on the rocks. Many of the symbols are simply made out of lines and shapes.

Materials

- print the pictographs and petroglyphs, pages 29 and 30 in *Art and Artists* PDF
- examples of symbols used in rock art

For each child:

- thick paper or thin tagboard— 4" x 6" (10 x 15 cm)
- brown construction paper— 9" x 12" (23 x 30.5 cm)
- black or brown printing ink
- oil pastels—brown, yellow, red, beige, gray, and white
- a pencil
- masking tape
- a brayer

Step by Step

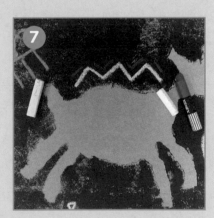

1. Give children the project materials. Then have them draw the outline of an animal of their choice in pencil on the thick paper or tagboard. Tell them that this is a contour drawing, so there should not be any details!

2. Next, have children carefully tear out their animal along the pencil line. This torn animal is a stencil.

3. Then, with a small piece of masking tape, have them attach their animal stencils to the center of the brown paper.

4. Have children roll an even amount of brown or black ink onto the paper with a brayer. The entire paper should be covered. After the paint dries, children will take off the animal stencil to reveal the brown animal shape below it.

5. Allow the papers to dry.

6. Further discuss petroglyphs and pictographs with children. The painted papers represent petroglyphs because the animal drawings are "carved" into the painted paper. Now have children add pictographs to their designs.

7. Lastly, have them use the oil pastels to add pictographs on the inked area of their paper.

Gargoyles

Medieval Architects and Builders

Medieval architects and builders included ornate gargoyles as part of the buildings they designed and built. Gargoyles are stone figures found mainly on the top of Gothic-style buildings. Because they were originally used as drains on castles and churches, the gargoyles' mouths were usually open.

Gargoyles were also believed to scare off evil spirits from the buildings they were placed upon. They fit in well with the ornate decoration of the time. Usually, gargoyles are in the form of made-up creatures.

Read More About the Art:

Gargoyles: 30 Postcards

Holy Terrors: Gargoyles on Medieval Buildings by Janetta Rebold Benton

Gargoyle

Talk About...

Show children the pictures of Gothic architecture and gargoyles. Talk about gargoyles with children.

Materials

- print the pictures of gargoyles and Gothic architecture, pages 31 and 32 in *Art and Artists* PDF

For each child:

- clay
- texture tools (nails, craft sticks, toothpicks, etc.)
- gray tempera paint
- a paintbrush

Step by Step

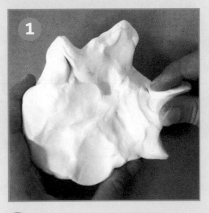

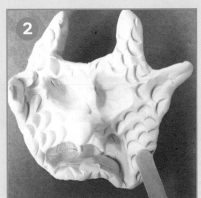

1. Give children the project materials. Then help them make gargoyles using a pinch-pull technique. Start each child off with a block or ball of clay. Keeping the clay all in one piece, children use their fingers to pull and pinch the clay into a creature. They might want to pull out legs, wings, and a head.

2. Encourage children to experiment with texture tools to press in and draw details on the basic gargoyle form. The head of a nail or the rounded end of a wooden craft stick make good scales when pressed in repeatedly.

3. Next, have children hollow out the bottom of their gargoyles so they can dry more quickly.

4. Tell them to add their names to the bottom of their gargoyles.

5. Allow the clay to dry and then fire or bake according to the clay manufacturer's directions.

6. Lastly, have children paint their gargoyles gray to make them look like stone.

CRAFTS and ART

ArtWorks for Kids

EMC 761
Grades 1–6

The 68 fun art experiences and projects introduce students to painting, weaving, working with clay, and more.

Art for All Seasons

EMC 2001
Grades 1–4

Your year-round source for art projects related to holidays and the four seasons.

Colorful Activity Books

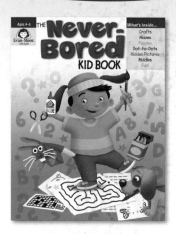

THE NEVER-BORED KID BOOK

Crafts, mazes, puzzles, word games, dot-to-dots, and more

Grades PreK–4

TOP STUDENT WORKBOOKS

Jumbo activity book covers every subject, plus STEM and more

Grades PreK–6

SKILL SHARPENERS: CRITICAL THINKING

Creative and critical thinking activities and hands-on projects

Grades PreK–6